Welcome

Grace to You
And Peace
From God Our Father
And The Lord Jesus Christ

Calvin
&
C. S. Lewis

Solving the Riddle of the Reformation

Jordan Ferrier

ISBN 978-1-479-10128-3
ISBN 1-479-10128-1

Second Edition

Cover by: Vicki Ferrier, Little Hands Legacies

For
My Saviour
Jesus

To
My Wife
Vicki

As Well As
My Heroes
Keegan & Connor

Table of Contents

CHAPTER ONE

"For now we see in a mirror dimly, but then face to face.
Now I know in part;
then I shall know fully, even as I have been fully known."
1 Corinthians 13:12 (ESV)

It has been over twenty years since I spent the summer working on a kibbutz in Israel. I was sixteen, and thinking that if I stayed an extra year in Israel as a volunteer on the kibbutz, I would still only be 18 when I graduated High School. I was living just a few miles from the sea of Galilee, and every evening was glorious after a scorching day with the temps in the hundreds. It would cool down and after dark we would go walking or stand around in small groups and talk nonsense. I can still recall in vivid detail when the subject of free will and predestination first came up. I remember having an immediate visceral response: "Why did God have us go through all of this if He didn't have to. Why not just create us in heaven?"

Of course, no one could really give any definitive answers on the subject. It was simply this point against that point, and this Bible verse against that Bible verse. Each side claimed to be using exegesis (deriving meaning from the text), and accused the other side of eisegesis (reading meaning into the text). What everyone did agree on was that somehow God was sovereign and man was responsible; However, this simply left the question unanswered: How is God sovereign and man responsible?

It would be several years before I read my first book on the subject. A friend of ours began attending a church that taught "Reformed Theology," and she sent my wife *Chosen by God*, by R.C. Sproul. This friend was very excited over the answers that Calvinism gave. Mainly that she finally felt accepted by God just as she was. That it was all God, that He had chosen her, and there was nothing for her to contribute to her salvation.

I read the book, and have re-read it several times. The theology and answers given in *Chosen by God*, simply did not satisfy me. I disagreed without having great explanations as to why. Not only did things not "feel" right, I engaged in a lot of seems to me theology. For instance, "It seems to me that if the decision is up to man, then man is in control, not God." "It seems to me, if it is all up to God, then God is the

7

author of evil." I began to read one book after another on the subject. I would vacillate between five point Calvinism and zero point Calvinism, and all points of numbers in-between.

I thought I had finally found the answers to my questions when the book *Chosen but Free*, by Norman Geisler came out. Finally, I had answers to my questions and could hold my own in a debate with a Calvinist. Geisler explained how Calvin himself did not agree with "Limited Atonement" but taught a "Universal Atonement" instead. Geisler called his position "Moderate Calvinism" and the view of Sproul, etc. "Extreme Calvinism."

I decided to write a book and prove to my Calvinist friends that Calvin did indeed believe in a universal atonement, that Jesus had died for all, not just for the elect. I ordered Calvin's "Institutes" and a set of his commentaries. I set up a file in my computer and named it "Saving Calvin from Reformed theology," and began typing out quotes from Calvin. This exercise in futility was fun for about three weeks. I was spending hours and hours reading Calvin, trying to find the answers to this thorny issue of sovereignty, free will, and the atonement of Christ.

Then I came across *A Treatise On The Eternal Predestination of God*, a document written by Calvin that sums up and defends his 'Institutes' against an attack by Albert Pighius and Georgius, an Italian monk. The more I read this Treatise and Calvin's commentaries, the more convinced I became that Calvin did not believe Jesus died for all, in fact, I had a very difficult time figuring out what it was that Calvin believed. I was sure of one thing though: Geisler was wrong about Calvin, which meant R. C. Sproul was teaching "Classical Calvinism" not "Extreme Calvinism". I reached the conclusion that John Calvin did teach a limited atonement, and it was his belief that all those Jesus died for would be saved; Therefore, there had to be people that Jesus did not die for, since some people would not be saved.

The next book I read was *The Potters Freedom*, by James White. White confirmed many of the beliefs I now had about Calvin. He deals with many of the quotes Geisler was using from Calvin in their entirety, and uses a nearly identical line of reasoning that I had used that convinced me that Calvin taught limited atonement (See PF, pp. 253 - 262). The back and forth discussion on Calvin's limited atonement really illustrates how deeply each side misunderstands the other. Most of the authors that I have read that discuss the five points of Calvinism: TULIP: (1) Total Depravity, (2) Unconditional Election, (3) Limited Atonement,

(4) Irresistible Grace, and (5) Perseverance of the Saints agree that the five points stand or fall together. With one caveat: If the fifth point is wrong, all five points are wrong; However, if all of the first four points are wrong, the fifth point can still be true. Another way to state this is that if any of the first four points are wrong, all four are wrong, yet the fifth can still be true.

There are three possible combinations:

First Possible Combination - All Five True:

Total Depravity -	True
Unconditional Election -	True
Limited Atonement -	True
Irresistible Grace -	True
Perseverance of the Saints -	True

Second Possible Combination - All Five False:

Total Depravity -	False
Unconditional Election -	False
Limited Atonement -	False
Irresistible Grace -	False
Perseverance of the Saints -	False

Third Possible Combination - First Four False, Fifth True

Total Depravity -	False
Unconditional Election -	False
Limited Atonement -	False
Irresistible Grace -	False
Perseverance of the Saints -	True

I also believe that if any of the first four points are correct, all five points are correct. Which means there can only be one kind of Calvinist...

This shows the importance of Limited Atonement which was the point of attack that Geisler had used in his book Chosen but Free, (CBF, appendix two). This view comes from a French Protestant pastor, Moses Amyrald, and Calvinists refer to his teachings as the "Amyraut Heresy." (CBF, p. 56) My guess as to why Geisler wants to hold onto Calvin as supporting his view is that he does not want to give up on sola gratia (grace alone) and sola fidei (faith alone). This is merely a guess from reading Geisler's Systematic Theology, where he says that the cry of the reformation was justification by faith alone. (ST 3, p. 258)

As I was reading all of these books, I was carrying on an email discussion about the same topic with some of my friends. I also led a group of guys through some of what I had learned, trying to lay out the different views held by "Calvinists" and "Arminians". When I began reading a list of books by C. S. Lewis, I began to finally understand Calvin and the reformed position. Both Calvin and C. S. Lewis share a belief in the authority of scripture, the sovereignty of God, and a faith in Jesus Christ. Both would affirm The Apostles Creed, The Nicene Creed, and The Athanasian Creed. The vexing riddle that has come out of the reformation was why two "protestants" would look at the same scriptures and come to radically different conclusions. It wasn't until I found the absolute foundational starting point of each man, that I came to understand why each believed the way they did.

I will attempt in the chapters to come to lay out side by side the belief system of Calvin and C. S. Lewis. I will try to explain what each one is saying, and then give the quotes from each man and his followers to support my explanations. The vast majority of what I say will not be new. It has been my experience that both sides misrepresent the opposing persons arguments because the two sides do not completely understand what the other is saying.

I believe that this study of the beliefs of Calvin and C. S. Lewis can bring unity to the body of Christ. Just as Jesus said:

"A new commandment I give to you, that you love one another: just as I have loved you, you also are to love one another. By this all people will know that you are My disciples, if you have love for one another." John 13 : 34 - 35 (ESV)

My intent is to bring the explanations along side each other in a way that makes both viewpoints understandable, no matter what your background or perspective. My hope is that this presentation will allow you to understand the riddle of the reformation and its solution. Instead of quoting Scriptures, pounding the pulpit, shouting exegesis!, and being frustrated with each other, a rational discussion of the actual issues can be undertaken.

If you happen to be like one of the Dwarves in "The Last Battle," (The Dwarfs are for the Dwarfs!) I hope that you too, will perceive the significance of these concepts, and realize a deeper understanding of God. If, by the grace of God, I have found the key to resolving the riddle of the reformation, it was due in part to a genuine desire to fully understand what each person was saying and why they were saying it. I ask that you put aside any conclusions you may already have made and "seek first to understand."

I love the following quotes by Abraham Joshua Heschel that drive this point home:

"The principle to be kept in mind is to know what we see, rather than to see what we know. Rather than blame things for being obscure, we should blame ourselves for being biased and prisoners of self-induced repetitiveness. Understanding (Divine Election) is an understanding of an understanding rather than an understanding of knowledge; it is exegesis of exegesis. It involves sharing the perspective from which the original understanding is done. Every mind operates with presuppositions or premises as well as within a particular way of thinking." (The Prophets, intro., pp. 9 - 13, Abridged, I substituted "Divine Election" in place of "Prophecy" in the original.)

The next chapter will describe an important area of agreement between John Calvin and C. S. Lewis.

CHAPTER TWO

"Now there are also many other things that Jesus did.
Were every one of them to be written,
I suppose that the world itself
could not contain the books that would be written."
John 21:25 (ESV)

Let's agree to avoid bibli-idolatry. The triune God is over and above the Scriptures. We do not worship The Bible -- instead we worship the God revealed in the Scriptures. The Holy Bible was written through the inspiration of the Holy Spirit, it is sufficient, and authoritative (2 Timothy 3:16 - 17). Yet, not only are there many books that have been written, every sermon -- in fact, every discussion about God -- is "commentary" on God and His revealed Word:

(MacDonald:) "Sad, indeed, would the whole matter be, if the Bible had told us everything God meant us to believe. But herein is the Bible itself greatly wronged. It nowhere lays claim to be regarded as *the* Word, *the* Way, *the* Truth. The Bible leads us to Jesus, the inexhaustible, the ever unfolding Revelation of God. It is Christ "in whom are hid all the treasures of wisdom and knowledge," not the Bible, save as leading to Him." (Unspoken Sermons, p. 18)

The Apostles creed, the Nicene creed, and the Athanasian creed are not found word for word in Scripture, but are used as the 'measuring sticks' of what is considered orthodox Christianity. It is incredibly valuable to read the writings of those that have gone before us in the faith. It would be ridiculous to ignore the work of previous generations and continually fight over the doctrine of the trinity and the deity of Christ. It is a simple matter to read the thoughts of those that dealt with these issues and to understand how the creeds they developed seamlessly match with Scripture.

Just as Scripture does not contain all Truth about God, Scripture also does not contain all Truth about our world. For example, the Pythagorean theorem used in mathematics is not found in Scripture, it is still true, and as Truth it belongs to God. It takes a rational being to interpret Scripture; Otherwise, we could simply open the Bible and set it in front of a squirrel and see what happens. Even then, we would need to be a rational being to derive any meaning from what we observed happen between the squirrel and the Scriptures.

Without the ability to reason, we do not have the capacity to read. "It is literally impossible to think without logic." (ST 1, p. 92) You would not be able to read this sentence, let alone the Scriptures, without the capacity to use reason to learn how to read the words.

Without a life with which to experience things, we would not be able to reason. We must exist as a rational soul, before we are able to use the laws of logic to be able to reason. Without reason, we would not be able to understand what it is that we are experiencing. The very words and sentences you are reading would have no meaning. Reason and experience are intertwined. Even now you are reasoning as you experience the words on this page.

C. S. Lewis describes the balance between logic and experience:

(Lewis:) "It is Reason herself which teaches us not to rely on Reason only in this matter. For Reason knows that she cannot work without materials. When it becomes clear that you cannot find out by reasoning whether the cat is in the linen-cupboard, it is Reason herself who whispers, 'Go and look. This is not my job: it is a matter for the senses'. So here. The materials for correcting our abstract conception of God cannot be supplied by Reason: she will be the first to tell you to go and try experience-- 'Oh, taste and see!' For of course she will have already pointed out that your present position is absurd." (Miracles, p. 259)

Logic is correct thought, while reason is putting logic to use correctly. If someone is "unreasonable" then they are not using logic correctly. They are going against common sense -- the laws of logic. I certainly will not be one to argue that God is unreasonable.

The use of reason as the basis of all thought, and use of logic as the basis of all correct thought does not put Calvin and C. S. Lewis in conflict with each other. The two agree on this. R.C. Sproul wrote:

(Sproul:) "I don't like contradictions. I find little comfort in them. I never cease to be amazed at the ease with which Christians seem to be comfortable with them. I hear statements like, "God is bigger than logic!" or "Faith is higher than reason!" to defend the use of contradictions in theology.

13

I certainly agree that God is bigger than logic and that faith is higher than reason. I agree with all my heart and with all my head. What I want to avoid is a God who is smaller than logic and a faith that is lower than reason. A God who is smaller than logic would be and should be destroyed by logic. A faith that is lower than reason is irrational and absurd." (CBG, p. 40)

(Sproul:) "For Christians to embrace both poles of a blatant contradiction is to commit intellectual suicide and to slander the Holy Spirit. The Holy Spirit is not the author of confusion. God does not speak with a forked tongue." (CBG, p. 41 - underline is mine)

(Sproul:) "Contradictions can never coexist, not even in the mind of God. If both poles of a genuine contradiction could be true in the mind of God, then nothing God ever revealed to us could possibly have any meaning. If good and evil, justice and injustice, righteousness and unrighteousness, Christ and Antichrist could all mean the same thing to God's mind, then truth of any kind would be utterly impossible." (CBG, p. 44 - underline is mine)

We should all wholeheartedly agree with this excellent description and use of logic!
C. S. Lewis complements R. C. Sproul:

(Lewis:) "…an open mind about the ultimate foundations either of Theoretical or of Practical Reason is idiocy. If a man's mind is open on these things, let his mouth at least be shut. He can say nothing to the purpose." (Abolition, p. 481)

To be able to reason correctly, we need to know the basic laws of logic. Aristotle discovered the laws of logic and systematized them. Here are a few of the most basic laws:

1. The law of non-contradiction: A is not non-A: God is not non-God: God is not the devil: No two contradictory statements can both be true at the same time and in the same sense.
2. The law of identity: A is A: God is God.
3. The law of the excluded middle: it is either A or non-A: It is either God or not God we are speaking about.

4. The law of rational inference: Valid inferences can be made from what is known to what is unknown, without this law, no one could prove any point.
(These fours points are found in: Reason, p. 16)

Norman Geisler and Ronald Brooks share some excellent insights into logic:

(Geisler:) "From the standpoint of reality, we understand that God is the basis of all logic. As the ultimate reality, all truth is ultimately found in Him. He has created the reality that we know and in which we have discovered the laws of logic. He has structured the world in such a way that these laws cannot be denied; however, we did not know God first and then learn logic from Him. He exists as the basis of all logic (in reality), but we discovered logic first and came to know God through it. This is true even if we came to know God through His revelation, because we understood the revelation through logic. In the order of being, God is first; but in the order of knowing, logic leads us to all knowledge of God. God is the basis of all logic (in the order of *being*), but logic is the basis of all knowledge of God (in the order of *knowing*)." (Reason, p. 17 - italics and parentheses in original)

(Geisler:) "It is true that in reality God is prior to everything else. In this sense, God is prior to logic in the order of being. Logic is a form of rational thought, and God is the ultimate rational Being. So ontologically (the study of being) logic is subject to God. However, this does not mean that logic is arbitrary -- God does not merely choose to be rational and consistent. *He is rational by His very nature.* The scriptures inform us, for example, "It is impossible for God to lie" (Hebrews 6:18) and that "He cannot deny Himself" (2 Timothy 2:13 NKJV). Likewise, God cannot be irrational. It is contrary to His nature as the ultimate, perfect, absolutely rational Being in the universe to violate the laws of logic." (ST 1, p. 90 - italics in original - "the study of being" added for explanation)

(Geisler:) "Logic is the necessary pre-condition for all rational thought. Rational thought is what separates man from animal, and it is the very thing that allows us to know and experience God. For example, I need a map before I can get to Chicago. But Chicago must exist before the map can help me get there. We use logic first to come to know God, but God exists first before we can know Him." (Reason, p. 17)

C. S. Lewis agrees with these statements about logic:

(Lewis:) "If the value of our reasoning is in doubt, you cannot try to establish it by reasoning. If a proof that there are no proofs is nonsensical, so is a proof that there are proofs. Reason is our starting point. There can be no question either of attacking or defending it. If by treating it as a mere phenomenon you put yourself outside it, there is then no way, except by begging the question, of getting inside again." (Miracles, p. 222 - underline is mine - note that "begging the question" is a logical fallacy which will be explained at the end of the chapter.)

(Geisler:) "While God is prior to logic in the order of being (ontologically), logic is prior to God in the order of knowing (epistemologically). No knowledge is possible without the laws of thought; if this is not true, then nothing else follows. Even the statement "God is God" makes no sense unless the law of identity holds (A is A). Likewise, the affirmation that "God exists" cannot be true if the law of non-contradiction is not binding, otherwise God could exist and not exist at the same time and in the same sense." (ST 1, p. 90 - parentheses and quotation marks in original)

I find the following quote a Truth of great worth. Read it over slowly. Savor the beauty of it. If it is beyond your comprehension now, we will come back to it again down the road. I believe you will easily see the treasure in this concept when the two opposing viewpoints are laid out:

(Geisler:) "This does not make God subject to something beyond Himself. When God is subject to good reason (logic), He is subject to His own nature (see Clark, CVMT), since He is the ultimate Reason or Logos (John 1:1). Likewise, when God is subject to the law of justice, He is not bound by something beyond Himself, but to something within Himself, which is His own unchangeable nature." (ST 1, p. 91)

Geisler explains how we should use logic in our study of God:

(Geisler:) "God is the author of all logic. So, technically speaking, God does not flow from logic; logic flows from God. It isn't God that we examine using logic; it is our statements about God. No one is trying to judge God. It is the statements or "commentary" that we make about Him that we analyze with logic. Logic simply provides a way to see if those statements are true -- if they fit with the reality of who God really is. Using logic in theology is simply applying God's test to our statements about God. It is God's way for us to come to the truth." (Reason, pp. 17 - 18)

(Geisler:) "Systematic Theology is a series of statements about God that, if true, inform us about Him. No statement about God can make any sense, to say nothing of being true, unless it abides by the undeniable rules of reason." (ST 1, p. 91)

The study of logic is not limited to what is correct reasoning, it also lists many errors that are cataloged as fallacies. For instance there is a logical fallacy called Petitio Principii, or "begging the question":

(Geisler:) "This is an argument where the conclusion is sneaked into the premises. "Accept this conclusion as true because the premise from which it comes is true." It is a circular argument, where the conclusion actually becomes a premise." (Reason, p. 100)

An example of "begging the question" would be that since the Bible says that:

"All scripture is given by inspiration of God, and is profitable for doctrine, for reproof, for correction, for instruction in righteousness." 2 Timothy 3 : 16 (KJV)

Then the Bible must be true; However:

(Geisler:) "By referring to the Bible as proof, there is an implicit assumption that the Bible has divine authority. But that is the very question being asked. You can't just say that the Bible says it came from God; so does the Koran, (and the book of Mormon). This assumed premise restates the conclusion and begs the question." (Reason, p. 100 - parenthetical statement is mine)

Of course this does not mean that the Bible is false, just that one of the arguments used is fallacious. There are many other fallacies which you can read about in a good book on the subject of logic. I recommend the one I have been quoting from: *Come let us Reason*, by Geisler and Brooks.

Geisler gives an excellent summary:

(Geisler:) "All Truth is *revealed* by God, whether in special or general revelation, but all truth is received by *reason*." (ST 1, p. 91 - italics in original) "While there may be objections to the use of logic, there is a difference between the use of good *reason*, which the Bible commends to *discover* truth (Isaiah 1:18; Matthew 22:37; 1 Peter 3:15), and the use of *rationalism* to *determine* truth, which Scripture does not commend. Good reason does not subject God to finite minds, but rather subjects our finite minds to His infinite Mind. (2 Cor. 10:5; 1 Cor. 1:21)." (ST 1, p. 91 - italics in original-underlined words are my addition)

Here are a couple of verses that illustrate the use of Scripture and Reason to arrive at the correct conclusion:

Matthew 19:26 "But Jesus looked at them and said, 'With man this is impossible, but with God all things are possible.' " (ESV)

Luke 1:37   "For nothing will be impossible with God." (ESV)

Hebrews 6:18 " ...it is impossible for God to lie..." (ESV)

It is obvious that lying is a thing, and since all things are possible for God, it would seem obvious that it is possible for God to lie; However, this directly contradicts Scripture which clearly states that it is impossible for God to lie. How can a thing -- lying -- be impossible for God to do, when nothing is impossible for God?

John 14:6 Jesus said to him, "I am the way, and the truth, and the life. No one comes to the Father, except through me." (ESV)

For God to be both the truth and a liar is impossible. A being that can be both the truth and a liar is not possible. To say that such a being could exist is nonsense. A being that is both the truth and liar is not a thing, it is a logical contradiction to state that such a thing could possibly exist. Scripture is correct that all things are possible for God, and no thing is impossible for God, a being that is both a liar and the truth is nonsense, and as nonsense, it is not a real thing.

In the next chapter I will present the foundational beliefs of Calvin and C. S. Lewis and show how each uses logic to derive a specific meaning from Scripture. While both Calvin and C. S. Lewis agree on the early creeds of Christianity, they each take a different view of how God's attribute of Omnipotence relates to the original sin of Adam and Eve. Each man uses Scripture and reason to arrive at a conclusion. These opposing conclusions are the starting point for each man's systematic theology. Each systematic theology is in almost complete opposition to the other. There is no way to reconcile the two.

CHAPTER THREE

"Whatever the LORD pleases, He does, in heaven and on earth, in the seas and all the deeps." Psalms 135:6 (ESV)
    &
"Our God is in the heavens; He does all that He pleases."
Psalms 115:3 (ESV)
    &
"For nothing is impossible with God." Luke 1:37 (NIV)

       It surprised me to find that both Calvin and C. S. Lewis have these verses at the starting point of their beliefs on Soteriology (salvation). The problem is really quite simple: If God is both Omnipotent and good, why did Lucifer and Adam sin? Either God wants to abolish evil, and cannot; or he can, but does not want to; or he cannot and does not want to. If he wants to, but cannot, he is impotent. If he can, and does not want to, he is wicked. But, if God both can and wants to abolish evil, then how comes evil into the world? ("Theodicy" is the term used to describe attempts to resolve this problem of evil.)

       I will begin by laying out the theodicy that "Classical Calvinism" or "Reformed Theology" uses to resolve this difficulty, and then builds on this base to systematize the rest of the Calvinistic view on Soteriology. The intent is to let the Calvinist position speak for itself by using quotes from Calvin, or those who accurately reflect his view. I will either give a brief introduction before the quotes, or a summary of the conclusions that can be drawn after the quotes.

R.C. Sproul presents the three foundational premises of Calvinism:

(Sproul:) "*If God is totally righteous, how could he have created a universe where evil is present? If all things come from God, doesn't evil come from him as well?* Then, as now, I realized that evil was a problem for the sovereignty of God. Did evil come into the world against God's sovereign will? If so, then He is not absolutely sovereign. If not, then we must conclude that is some sense even evil is foreordained by God." (CBG, pp. 28 - 29 - italics in original)

(Sproul:) "A frequent objection we hear is that if God knew in advance that we were going to sin, why did He create us in the first place? One philosopher stated the problem this way: "If God knew we would sin but could not stop it, then He is neither omnipotent nor sovereign. If He could stop it but chose not to, then He is neither loving nor benevolent." By this approach God is made to look bad no matter how we answer the question.

We must assume that God knew in advance that man would fall. We also must assume that He could have intervened to stop it. Or He could have chosen not to create us at all. We grant all those hypothetical possibilities." (CBG, p. 32 - Underline is mine)

To summarize R.C. Sproul:
1. An Omniscient God would know in advance that man would fall.
2. An Omnipotent God could have intervened to stop the fall.
3. A Perfect God would not need to create man at all.

Calvin agrees with Sproul's first point that an Omniscient God would know that man would fall:

(Calvin:) "God foresaw the fall of Adam, and most certainly His suffering him to fall was not contrary to, but according to, His Divine will!" (EPG, p. 76)

In the following quote, Calvin agrees with Sproul's first and second point: that an Omniscient God knew Adam would fall, and an Omnipotent God could have stopped Adam from falling:

(Calvin:) "And if the matter be carried higher, and a question be moved concerning the first creation of man, Augustine meets that question thus: "We most wholesomely confess, that which we most rightly believe: that God, the Lord of all things, who created all things 'very good,' foreknew, that evil would arise out of this good: and He also knew, that it was more to the glory of His omnipotent goodness, to bring good out of evil, than not to permit evil to be at all!" (EPG, p. 25 - underline is mine)

A second quote where Calvin teaches that an Omnipotent God could have stopped the fall of Adam:

(Calvin:) "Wherefore, as far as these natures themselves were concerned, *they* did what they did, contrary to the will of God: but, as far as the omnipotence of God is concerned, <u>they acted according to His will</u>: <u>nor could they have acted contrary to it</u>." (EPG, p. 26 - italics in original - underline is mine)

Calvin quotes Augustine again, and they explain that the premises that God knew Adam would fall, and that God could have stopped Adam from sinning are the foundation of their theology:

(Calvin:) "Although, therefore, those things which are evil, in so far as they are evil, are not good: yet it *is good*, that there should not only be good things, but evil things also. For, unless there were this good, --that evil things also existed: those <u>evil things would not be permitted, by the Great and Good Omnipotent, to exist at all</u>. <u>For He, without doubt, can as easily refuse to permit to be done what He does not will to be done</u>, as He can do that which He wills to be done. <u>Unless we fully believe this</u>, <u>the very beginning of our faith is periled: by which, we profess to believe in God ALMIGHTY!</u>" (EPG, pp. 25 - 26 - underline is mine - Capitalization and italics in original)

While Sproul wrote that we must assume that God could have intervened to stop the fall, Augustine and Calvin explain how God could have stopped the fall: By over-ruling Adam's decision to disobey.
Around the year 1070, Anselm of Canterbury wrote that God is "that than which nothing greater can be conceived." For example, the greatest amount of power than man can conceive of God having is all power; Therefore, God is Omnipotent. The greatest amount of knowledge that God can be conceived of having is for God to be all-knowing; Therefore, God is Omniscient. This line of reasoning can be used for many of the attributes of God, but for Calvin's theology, the most important attributes of God are Omnipotence and Freedom or Liberty.
Using Anselm's proposition: God is the most free being; Therefore, God has the most freedom of any being, and God is the freest being we can conceive of. This 'freedom' is often expressed in Calvin's theology as Sovereignty.

(Calvin:) "But as it would be utterly absurd to hold, that anything could be done *contrary* to the will of God; seeing that God is at Divine liberty to prevent that which He does not will to be done." "Whereas, Augustine proves, by this very argument, that everything that is done on earth, is effectually ruled, and over-ruled, by this *secret providence* of God! Nor does he hesitate to conclude, that everything that is done, is done by the *WILL OF GOD*! According to which conclusion, the Psalmist testifies, that God, sitting in heaven, doth what He will, "But our God, (saith the Psalmist,) is in the heavens: He hath done whatsoever He hath pleased." (Ps. 155:3.)" (EPG, p. 190 - italics and capitalization in original)

According to Calvin, since God is Omnipotent and Sovereign, He is free to over-rule any decision or action of any of His creatures at any time. If God chooses not to over-rule His creature, then God permitted the decision or action: Calvin quotes Augustine: "Nothing, therefore, is done, but that which the Omnipotent *willed* to be done, either by permitting it to be done, or by doing it Himself." (EPG, p. 25 - italics in original)

(Calvin:) "God does not only permit a thing to be done, or to continue, by His longsuffering, but He rules and over-rules what is done by His Almighty power." (EPG, p. 60 - underline is mine)

Since God was free to over-rule the sin of Adam, God by His permissive will must have permitted Adam to sin, thus permitting evil to exist: A repeat of Calvin and Augustine: "For, unless there were this good, --that evil things also existed; those evil things would not be permitted, by the Great and Good Omnipotent, to exist at all. For He, without doubt, can as easily refuse to permit to be done what He does not will to be done, as He can do that which He wills to be done. Unless we fully believe this, the very beginning of our faith is perilled: by which, we profess to believe in God ALMIGHTY!" (EPG, pp. 25 - 26 - underline is mine.)

Starting with "the very beginning of our faith", Calvin teaches the following six points:
1. God must always retain the right to over-rule any of His creatures' decisions at all times, or God is not Omnipotent and Sovereign.
(Calvin:) "Wherefore, we are to rest assured, that no *human wills* can resist the *will* of God, who doeth, according to His will, all things, in heaven and in earth; and who *has already* done, *by His will*, the things that *shall be* done. No will of men, we repeat, can resist the will of God, so as to prevent Him from doing what He willeth; seeing that He doeth

what He *will*, with the *wills* themselves of all mankind." (EPG, p. 134 - italics in original)

2. Adam & Eve had free-will ("free-will" is defined in point #3 and #4)

(Calvin:) "He so ordained the lives of angels and of men that He might first show, in them, what free-will could do." (EPG, p. 25)

(Calvin:) "He fell by his own full free-will; and by his own willing act." (EPG, p. 76)

(Sproul:) "Calvinism sees Adam sinning by his own free-will, not by divine coercion." (CBG, p. 97)

3. Free-will was a good gift to Adam & Eve.

(Sproul:) "Free-will is a good thing. That God gave us free-will does not cast blame on Him. In creation man was given an ability to sin and an ability not to sin." (CBG, p. 30)

(Calvin:) (agrees with Pighius:) "God wished to create a rational creature, capable of receiving that goodness: which could not be done without His bestowing on that creature freedom of will." (EPG, p. 70)

4. Free-will is: The ability to sin and the ability to not sin. Adam was created with free-will: "perfectly upright," "with the light of reason and with rectitude of nature."

(Calvin:) "I have everywhere asserted, that man was created, in the beginning, perfectly upright." (EPG, p. 112)

(Calvin:) "Adam was perfect, and could do, perfectly." (EPG, p. 114)

(Calvin:) "Man, that he might be the image of God, was adorned from the first with the light of reason and with rectitude of nature." (EPG, p. 71 - Rectitude: Rightness of principle or conduct, moral virtue: Correctness: Straightness.)

5. The fall was sin. Sin is evil. The fall was evil.

Romans 5:12: "just as sin came into the world through one man" (ESV)

(Sproul:) "sin...is evil" (CBG, p. 31)

(Calvin:) "For we well know, that nothing is more contrary to the nature of God, than sin." (EPG, p. 187)

6. The tree of the knowledge of good and evil was a test of obedience. Adam and Eve, while having free-will, were still under the rule of God. God used the tree of the knowledge of good and evil to give Adam and Eve free-will.

(Calvin:) "Therefore, the prohibition of one tree was a test of obedience." (Commentary on Genesis, p. 125 - 126)

(Calvin:) "Therefore, abstinence from the fruit of one tree was a kind of first lesson in obedience, that man might know he had a Director and Lord of his life, on whose will he ought to depend, and in whose commands he ought to acquiesce." (Genesis, p. 126)

(Calvin:) "But at the time of which we speak, a precept was given to man, whence he might know that God ruled over him." (Genesis, p. 126)

(Calvin:) "Wherefore, when God commands Adam not to taste the fruit of the "tree of knowledge of good and evil;" He thereby tests his obedience." (EPG, p. 185)

To recap the six points without the supporting quotes:
1. God must always retain the right to over-rule any of His creatures' decisions at all times, or God is not Omnipotent and Sovereign.
2. Adam and Eve had "free-will".
3. Free-will was a good gift to Adam and Eve.
4. Free-will is: The ability to sin and the ability to not sin.
5. The fall was sin. Sin is evil. The fall was evil.
6. The tree of the knowledge of good and evil was a test of obedience.

It is clear from Scripture that Adam sinned, disobeyed God, did evil, and fell:

(Calvin:) "But as it would be utterly absurd to hold, that anything could be done *contrary* to the will of God; seeing that God is at Divine liberty to prevent that which He does not will to be done." "...Augustine proves ... that everything that is done on earth, is effectually ruled, and over-ruled, by this *secret providence* of God! Nor does he hesitate to conclude, that everything that is done, is done by the *WILL OF GOD!*" (EPG, p. 190 - italics in original).

Since the fall of Adam happened, the fall must have been according to the secret providence and will of God:

(Calvin:) "Augustine testifies, --'God, in a secret and marvellous way, *justly wills*, the things which men *unjustly* do'. " (EPG, p. 179 - italics in original)

(Calvin:) "God foresaw the fall of Adam, and most certainly His suffering him to fall was not contrary to, but according to, His Divine will!" (EPG, p. 76)

The manner in which an Omnipotent God would have stopped Adam and Eve from sinning is that an Absolutely Sovereign Omnipotent God could have over-ruled Adam and Eve's decision to sin and fall, that an Omniscient God would know that men would sin, a Omnipotent God could have stopped Adam from sinning, and a Perfect God did not have to create man at all.

The chart below illustrates what Augustine and Calvin call "the very beginning of our faith":

The points between the dotted lines will be used throughout the book to illustrate how Reformed Theology is an interlocking system of belief. As the discussion progresses, additional points will be added:

Foundation of Reformed Theology / Calvinism:

1. God is free to over-rule any of His creatures' decisions.
2.   A. God is Omniscient
B. God is Omnipotent
C. God is Perfect
3.   A. God knew the fall would happen.
    B. God could have stopped the fall from happening
    C. God did not need to create anything.

4. The fall was willed, ordained, and decreed by God > Everything
   that happens is the will of God.

Reformed Theology is a systematic Theology. It interlocks from end to end. I like to think of it as a braided rope. All of the threads in the rope are intertwined and inseparable from one another. A rope only unravels from one of the ends, which is why we often see the ends of rope burned to fuse the ends together. It is of utmost importance to ensure that the foundation of your theological system is correct. I am not saying that the foundation of Reformed Theology is that an Omnipotent God could have stopped Adam and Eve from sinning -- Augustine, Calvin, and Sproul are all saying it. This is where they say to begin. I agree that this is the correct place to begin. C. S. Lewis will also agree that this is the correct starting point.

Let's examine these three foundational statements using the laws of logic we agreed on in the last chapter using the following structure: A rational being experiences God as revealed in the Scriptures. From this revelation we derive truth statements about God which we call "Theology". From these theological statements man draws a meaning to develop a "philosophy". These statements of meaning are examined by Logic / Reason to determine if they are Orthodox beliefs or correct thinking.

1. Calvinists read in scripture that God is Omniscient. This means that God knew that man would sin. If God did not know man would sin then God is not Omniscient. <u>God knew in advance that man would sin.</u>

2. Calvinists read in scripture that God is Omnipotent. This means that God could have prevented man from sinning. If God could not have prevented man from sinning then God is not Omnipotent. <u>Everything that happens is the will of God and it must have been God's will that man sin.</u>

3. Calvinists read in Scripture that God is Perfect. This means that God did not need to create man. If God is perfect apart from His creation, there is no need for God to create. <u>God could have chose to not create man.</u>

Calvin and Augustine call these three propositions the "beginning

27

of our faith" while R.C. Sproul simply calls them assumptions. These three men are correct when they point out that it is these three philosophical presuppositions upon which all of Calvinism is built. The following quote is taken from a conference in which R. C. Sproul, Albert Mohler, and Ravi Zacharias were answering questions from an audience. Sproul will give a summary of the origin of evil and put the second principle listed above to use:

(Sproul:) "When evil comes into the world by God's design and by God's sovereign will -- evil is truly evil and it is a sin to call evil good, or good evil -- but when God decrees that evil should occur, it is good that it occurs, that is the whole point that has been spoken here, that even though evil is evil, it is good that evil exists, or it couldn't be here, because God ordains it and God is altogether good and He only ordains that which is good. Evil is evil, but it is good that it is here or He would not ordain it. That is not too difficult." (Sproul, National Conference, 2007)

This explanation agrees with the previous quote where Augustine wrote:

(Calvin / Augustine:) "And He also knew, that it was more to the glory of His Omnipotent goodness, to bring good out of evil, than not to permit evil to be at all!" (EPG, p. 25)

Martin Luther is also in agreement and makes an appeal to reason / logic as a proof that this foundational view is correct:

(Luther:) "For if we believe it to be true, that God foreknows and fore-ordains all things; that He can be neither deceived nor hindered in His Prescience and predestination; and that nothing can take place but according to His Will, (which reason herself is compelled to confess;) then, even according to the testimony of reason herself, there can be no "Free-will" --in man, --in angel, --or in any creature!" (Bondage, p. 390 - underline is mine)

Augustine, Luther, Calvin, and Sproul are unified in this view of God and the fall of man. Calvinism has far more than the five "TULIP" points. These first points are the real basis of the systematic theology of

Calvin. The traditional five points of Calvinism are built upon this foundation. This foundation is "the perspective from which the original understanding is done". Before we move on to show how the rest of Calvinism is built on this foundation, I will explain how C. S. Lewis has a different view of the same scriptures, which leads to an opposing foundation and system of belief. First, I will list the scriptures from the beginning of the chapter:

"Whatever the LORD pleases, He does, in heaven and on earth, in the seas and all the deeps." Psalms 135:6 (ESV)

"Our God is in the heavens; He does all that He pleases." Psalms 115:3 (ESV)

"For nothing is impossible with God." Luke 1:37 (NIV)

There are several more scriptures that address the same issue, but show that there are things that it does not please God to do, or that it is impossible for God to do, such as lie:

"So when God desired to show more convincingly to the heirs of the promise the unchangeable character of his purpose, he guaranteed it with an oath, so that by two unchangeable things, in which it is impossible for God to lie, we who have fled for refuge might have strong encouragement to hold fast to the hope set before us." Hebrews 6:17 - 18 (ESV - underline is mine)

The eyes of God are too pure to look at evil. It is impossible for God to see evil and look upon wrong:

"Are you not from everlasting, O LORD my God, my Holy One? We shall not die. O LORD, you have ordained them as a judgment, and you, O Rock, have established them for reproof. You who are of purer eyes than to see evil and cannot look at wrong, why do you idly look at traitors and remain silent when the wicked swallows up the man more righteous than he?" Habakkuk 1:12 - 13 (ESV - underline is mine)
It is impossible for God to deny Himself:

"The saying is trustworthy, for: If we have died with Him, we will also live with Him; if we endure, we will also reign with Him; if we deny Him, He also will deny us; if we are faithless, He remains faithful-- <u>for He cannot deny Himself</u>." 2 Timothy 2:11 -13 (ESV - underline is mine)

God cannot be tempted with evil, and God cannot tempt man:

"Let no one say when he is tempted, "I am being tempted by God," for <u>God cannot be tempted with evil</u>, <u>and He Himself tempts no one</u>." James 1:13 (ESV - underline is mine)

Returning to Anselm's proposition which both Calvin and C. S. Lewis agree with: God is the most free being; Therefore, God has the most freedom of any being, and God is the freest being we can conceive of.

If God must be able, at all times, to over-rule any of His creatures' decisions or actions, then God is free to do anything except give freedom to any of His creatures. Calvin's view of the freedom and Omnipotence of God leads to the conclusion that God is free to do anything except give real freedom to His creatures. This ultimately means that God is not free to give real freedom to His creatures. For Anselm's premise that God is "that than which nothing greater can be conceived" to be correct, then God is the freest Being, and as the freest Being, God is free to give real freedom to His creatures.

Calvin's first point, presented at the beginning of this introduction was: 1. God is the most free being, or, God is more free than man. God must always retain the right to over-rule any of His creatures' decisions at all times, or God is not Omnipotent and Sovereign.

(Sproul:) "I once read a statement by a Christian who said, "God's sovereignty can never restrict human freedom." Imagine a Christian thinker making such a statement. This is sheer humanism." (CBG, p. 42)

The argument is: God is free to stop any man at any time from doing anything, or else God is not sovereign. God is free to stop any man at any time from doing anything, or else man is more free than God.

If God is not free to stop man, then man is doing something that God cannot stop, which means that God is not sovereign, as well as, God is not as free as man (or man is more free than God), and God is reacting to man.

(Sproul:) "God is free. I am free. God is more free than I am. If my freedom runs up against God's freedom, I lose. His freedom restricts mine; my freedom does not restrict his." (CBG, p. 43)

This is Sproul's argument, that if God could not stop Adam from sinning, then Adam was more free than God.
The first philosophical presupposition of Reformed Theology is stated thus:
1. God is free to do anything, except give real freedom to one of His creatures.
OR
1. God is not free to give real freedom to one of His creatures (since God would no longer be absolutely Sovereign).

This philosophical presupposition violates points 2, 3, & 4, which Augustine, Calvin and Sproul all teach. (2. Adam and Eve had free-will. 3. Free-will was a good gift to Adam and Eve. 4. Free-will is the ability to sin and the ability to not sin.) This philosophical presupposition is also contrary to Scripture: Specifically Gen 2:16 - 17, where Scripture teaches that God is free to give real freedom to His creatures, and God did give real freedom to His creatures, when God told Adam that he was free to eat from any tree.
C. S. Lewis would agree with all of Calvin's six points except the first. The first point would say:
1. As Sovereign over His creation, God is free to give real freedom to His creatures, and He did so, in Genesis 2:16 - 17.

The following is Chapter Two from "The Problem of Pain" by C. S. Lewis. "DIVINE OMNIPOTENCE" is the chapter heading. C. S. Lewis will state his case with one short quote from Saint Thomas Aquinas and four simple paragraphs:

(Lewis:) "Nothing which implies contradiction falls under the omnipotence of God. THOMAS AQUINAS, Summ. Theol., IA Q XXV, ART 4"
(Lewis:) " 'If God were good, He would wish to make His creatures

perfectly happy, and if God were almighty, He would be able to do what He wished. But the creatures are not happy. Therefore God lacks either goodness, or power, or both.' This is the problem of pain, in its simplest form. The possibility of answering it depends on showing that the terms 'good' and 'almighty', and perhaps also the term 'happy', are equivocal: for it must be admitted from the outset that if the popular meanings attached to these words are the best, or the only possible, meanings, then the argument is unanswerable. In this chapter I shall make some comments on the idea of Omnipotence, and, in the following, some on the idea of Goodness."

"*Omnipotence* means 'power to do all, or everything'. (The original meaning in Latin may have been 'power *over* or *in* all'. I give what I take to be the current sense.) And we are told in Scripture that 'with God all things are possible'. It is common enough, in argument with an unbeliever, to be told that God, if He existed and were good, would do this or that; and then, if we point out that the proposed action is impossible, to be met with the retort 'But I thought God was supposed to be able to do anything'. This raises the whole question of impossibility.

"In ordinary usage the word *impossible* generally implies a suppressed clause beginning with the word *unless*. Thus it is impossible for me to see the street from where I sit writing at this moment; that is, it is impossible to see the street *unless* I go up to the top floor where I shall be high enough to overlook the intervening building. If I had broken my leg I should say 'But it is impossible to go up to the top floor' -- meaning, however, that it is impossible *unless* some friends turn up who will carry me. Now let us advance to a different plane of impossibility, by saying 'It is, at any rate, impossible to see the street *so long as* I remain where I am and the intervening building remains where it is.' Someone might add 'unless the nature of space, or of vision, were different from what it is'. I do not know what the best philosophers and scientists would say to this, but I should have to reply 'I don't know whether space and vision *could possibly* have been of such a nature as you suggest.' Now it is clear that the words *could possibly* here refer to some absolute kind of possibility or impossibility which is different from the relative possibilities and impossibilities we have been considering. I cannot say whether seeing round corners is, in this new sense, possible or not, because I do not know whether it is self-contradictory or not. <u>But I know very well that if it is self-contradictory it is absolutely impossible</u>. The absolutely impossible may also be called the intrinsically impossible because it carries its impossibility within itself, instead of borrowing it from other impossibilities which in their turn depend upon others. It has no *unless* clause attached to it. <u>It is impossible under all conditions and in all worlds and for all agents.</u>"

" 'All agents' here includes God Himself. His Omnipotence means power to do all that is intrinsically possible, not to do the intrinsically impossible. You may attribute miracles to Him, but not nonsense. This is no limit to His power. <u>If you choose to say 'God can give a creature free will and at the same time withhold free will from it', you have not succeeded in saying *anything* about God:</u> meaningless combinations of words do not suddenly acquire meaning simply because we prefix to them the two other words 'God can'. It remains true that all *things* are possible with God: the intrinsic impossibilities are not things but nonentities. It is no more possible for God than for the weakest of His creatures to carry out both of two mutually exclusive alternatives; not because His power meets an obstacle, but because nonsense remains nonsense even when we talk it about God." (POP, pp. 379 - 380 - italics in original - underline is mine)

C. S. Lewis agrees with Calvinists that God is Omniscient, Omnipotent, and Perfect. Lewis uses scripture to dispute the founding assumption of Calvinism that an Omnipotent God could have intervened to stop the fall since that would mean God could do what is logically contradictory. Genesis 2:16 - 17 speaks to the issue of God giving man freedom in the garden:

Genesis 2:16 - 17: "And the LORD God commanded the man, saying, Of every tree of the garden thou mayest freely eat: But of the tree of the knowledge of good and evil, thou shalt not eat of it: for in the day that thou eatest thereof thou shalt surely die." (KJV)

Genesis 2:16 - 17: "And the LORD God commanded the man, saying, "You may surely eat of every tree of the garden, but of the tree of the knowledge of good and evil you shall not eat, for in the day that you eat of it you shall surely die." (ESV)

Genesis 2:16 - 17 "And the LORD God commanded the man, "You are free to eat from any tree in the garden; but you must not eat from the tree of the knowledge of good and evil, for when you eat of it you will surely die." (NIV)

While Calvin and C. S. Lewis disagree on the first point, they agree on points 2 - 6:

Calvin:
1. Being Omnipotent, God is able to over-rule any of His creatures decisions or actions. God is free to do anything, except give freedom from being over-ruled to His creatures.

Lewis:
1. Being Omnipotent, God is free to give real freedom to His creatures, and He did so in Genesis 2:16 - 17.

Calvin & Lewis agree:
2. Adam & Eve had free-will.
3. Free-will was a good gift to Adam & Eve.
4. Free-will is: The ability to sin and the ability to not sin.
5. The fall was sin. Sin is evil. The fall was evil.
6. The tree of the knowledge of good and evil was a test of obedience. Adam and Eve, while having free-will, were still under the rule of God. God used the tree of the knowledge of good and evil to give Adam and Eve free-will.

There are three considerations or questions that need to be addressed at this point:
1. God stopped Abimelech from sinning, so why couldn't He have stopped Adam from sinning?
2. Did God want to stop Adam from sinning?
3. Could God have stopped Adam from sinning?

Question 1: Since God stopped Abimelech from sinning, could He have stopped Adam from sinning?

"From there Abraham journeyed toward the territory of the Negeb and lived between Kadesh and Shur; and he sojourned in Gerar.
And Abraham said of Sarah his wife, "She is my sister." And Abimelech king of Gerar sent and took Sarah.
But God came to Abimelech in a dream by night and said to him,

"Behold, you are a dead man because of the woman whom you have taken, for she is a man's wife."
Now Abimelech had not approached her. So he said, "Lord, will you kill an innocent people?
Did he not himself say to me, 'She is my sister'? And she herself said, 'He is my brother.' In the integrity of my heart and the innocence of my hands I have done this."
Then God said to him in the dream, "Yes, I know that you have done this in the integrity of your heart, and it was I who kept you from sinning against me. Therefore I did not let you touch her." Genesis 20:1 - 6 (ESV)

God did not tell Abimelech that he was free to be with Sarah before God stopped Abimelech from sinning with Sarah. God did tell Adam that he was free to eat from the tree of the knowledge of Good and Evil.

The five points that Calvin and C. S. Lewis agree on that applied to Adam, do not apply to Abimelech. Comparing an un-fallen Adam to a post-fall Abimelech is to commit the logical fallacy of a weak analogy. It is a simple 'category mistake' to compare Abimelech, from the category of fallen creatures, with Adam and Eve, from the category of un-fallen creatures. We need to remember to not confuse the 'rules' that apply to a fallen creature with the 'rules' that apply to an un-fallen creature.

C. S. Lewis agrees with R. C. Sproul when Sproul writes that "pre-fall man was able to sin" and "pre-fall man was able not to sin." (CBG, p. 66) C. S. Lewis specifically addresses this when he writes: "If you choose to say 'God can give a creature free will and at the same time withhold free will from it', you have not succeeded in saying *anything* about God."

God told man that he was free to eat from every tree, to prevent man from having the opportunity to eat from the tree would have made God a liar since man would not have really been free to eat from any tree. To say that God could give man the freedom to eat from the tree and then withhold that freedom from man would be to say that God can do what is logically contradictory. To say that God gave man the freedom to not eat from the tree, and then God ordained or willed man to eat from the tree is also logically contradictory.

Calvin tells us that Adam "was created, in the beginning, perfectly upright." Sproul agrees that "In creation man was given an ability to sin and an ability not to sin."

Then, Calvin tells us that God willed the fall to happen: "But it could not be otherwise, Adam could not but fall; according to the foreknowledge, and will of God." (EPG, p. 76)

(Sproul:) "We know that God is sovereign because we know that God is God. Therefore we must conclude that God foreordained sin. What else can we conclude?" (CBG, p. 31)

What happened to free-will and the ability to not sin?

(Lewis:) "not even Omnipotence can do what is self-contradictory." (Miracles, p. 241)

It is logically contradictory to say that God gave Adam the ability to sin and then say that God could withhold the ability to sin from Adam at the same time and in the same sense.

It is logically contradictory to say that God gave Adam the 'ability to NOT sin' and then to say that God withheld Adam's 'ability to not sin' at the same time and in the same sense. Which is exactly what Calvin teaches when he writes that "Adam could not but fall; according to the foreknowledge, and will of God". It is logically contradictory to say that God gave "rectitude of nature" and "free-will" to Adam, and then say that God would have still been able to over-rule Adam's decisions and actions.

Question 2: Did God want to stop Adam from sinning?

In Genesis 2:17, God commanded Adam to not eat from the tree of the knowledge of good and evil.

In Leviticus 19:18, God gives the command to "Love your neighbor as yourself" for the first of many times.

In Ephesians 5:25, God commands, "Husbands, love your wives, just as Christ loved the church and gave Himself up for her."

It seems reasonable to conclude from Scripture that if I believe that God wanted Adam to sin, then I would also have to conclude that God wants me to hate my neighbor and beat my wife. Instead God commands Adam to not sin, and commands us to love our neighbor and our wife. God did not want Adam to sin, just as He does not want you to hate your neighbor and beat your wife.

Question 3: Since God did not want Adam to disobey, could God have stopped Adam from sinning?

God told Adam he was free to eat from any tree, which is how God gave the good gift of free-will to Adam, and set up the test of obedience. To stop Adam from sinning, God would have to make Himself into a liar by telling Adam that he was free to eat from the tree of the knowledge of good and evil and then withhold that freedom from Adam. This is no insult to the Omnipotence of God, since not even Omnipotence can do that which is logically contradictory: give free-will and withhold free-will at the same time and in the same sense.

The six points presented above, can all be supported by Scripture as well as by Reason. Once these six points are agreed upon, it is clear that God could not stop Adam from sinning after Genesis 2:16 - 17. Knowing that something is going to happen does not make you responsible for it if you cannot stop it from happening. For you or I to say that the sun came up this morning by our "permissive will" is to imply that we could have stopped the sun from rising. I no more gave my permission for the sun to rise this morning than God gave His permission for Adam to sin. It is contrary to Scripture to believe that God wanted Adam to sin, that God could have stopped Adam from sinning, or that Adam sinned according to the will of God.

As Calvin teaches: The fall was sin. Sin is evil. The fall was evil. If God "willed" the fall to happen then God willed evil to happen. Calvin teaches that God wills evil to happen: "God, in a secret and marvellous way, *justly wills*, the things which men *unjustly* do." (EPG, p. 179 - italics in original) "Although God and the devil *will* the *same thing*: they do so in an utterly *different manner*." (EPG, p. 182 - italics in original)

It is Luther who says: "nothing can take place but according to His Will" and Calvin agrees: "Nothing, therefore, is done, but that which the Omnipotent *willed* to be done, either by permitting it to be done, or by doing it Himself." (EPG, p. 25 - italics in original)

According to Luther and Calvin, since evil happens, and nothing can take place but according to the will of God, God must will evil to happen.
1. God ordained and willed the fall to happen.
2. The fall was evil.
3. God willed evil to happen.

May I simply point out that:
1. If God wills evil to happen.
2. (and) What God wills is good.
3. Then evil is good.

God wills evil to happen, and what God wills is good, then evil is good.

I would rather agree with Scripture that the fruit of the tree of the knowledge of good and evil was the forbidden fruit, not the permitted fruit. Adam sinned against the command and will of God, not by God's permission and permissive will.

Remember in chapter two where R. C. Sproul explained: "<u>For Christians to embrace both poles of a blatant contradiction is to commit intellectual suicide and to slander the Holy Spirit</u>. The Holy Spirit is not the author of confusion. God does not speak with a forked tongue." (CBG, p. 41 - underline is mine)

When Reformed theology teaches that God gave Adam the good gift of free-will and rectitude, specifically the ability to sin and the ability to not sin, then also teaches that God could have over-ruled Adam's free decisions, Reformed theology embraces two poles of a blatant contradiction.

This logically contradictory system of belief leads to Reformed theology teaching that everything that happens is the will of God, and since evil happened (and is happening), that God wills evil to happen. God wills evil to happen, and what God wills is good; Therefore, evil is good. R. C. Sproul is correct: Embracing two poles of a blatant contradiction leads to intellectual suicide and slander of the Holy Spirit. In this case, it also ends with slander of God the Father by teaching that God views evil as being good. Ultimately, Calvinism is based on an "It seems to me" assumption: It seems to me that an Omnipotent God could have over-ruled Adam's decision to sin. Instead of "Sola Scriptura," Calvinism is reduced to a man-made religion based on "It seems to me" theology. By insisting that God must always retain the right to over-rule His creatures, Calvinism strips God of His divine liberty to give real freedom to any of His creatures.

The truth is often easier to understand when it is contrasted against the opposing argument which has been shown to be erroneous. Thankfully, just as God is always working to bring good out of evil, we can use the errors of Reformed theology to help us find the correct view of the origin of evil and the Sovereignty of God.

Foundation of Classical Theism:
1. God is free to give freedom to His creatures.
2.   A. God is Omniscient
       B. God is Omnipotent
       C. God is Perfect
3.   A. God knew the fall would happen.
       B. God could not stop the fall from happening.
       C. God did not need to create anything.
4. The fall was not ordained by God > God chose to give man
   the ability to choose.

Calvin quotes from Augustine's "Manual" to Laurentius where Augustine says: "How sure, how immutable, how all-efficacious is the will of God: --how many things He could do, or has power to do, which He wills not to do: (but that He wills nothing which He has not power to do)." (EPG, p. 25) C. S. Lewis agrees with Augustine and Aquinas, that God cannot do what is logically contradictory: "His Omnipotence means power to do all that is intrinsically possible, not to do the intrinsically impossible. You may attribute miracles to Him, but not nonsense. This is no limit to His power." (POP, p. 380).

C. S. Lewis agrees with Calvinists on the attributes of Omniscience and Perfection. The disagreement is on the meaning drawn from what an Omnipotent God can do. C. S. Lewis does not agree that God could have prevented man from having an opportunity to sin, since that would mean God did something that is logically contradictory.
1. God gave man the freedom to sin, and the ability to not sin.
2. If man is free to sin, God could not prevent man from sinning when the opportunity to sin was presented by Satan.

C. S. Lewis also does not agree that God willed, or ordained, the fall of man, since that would mean that God did something logically contradictory:
1. God gave man the freedom to sin, and the ability to not sin.
2. If man is free to not sin, God could not make man sin.

The next paragraph examines the meaning C. S. Lewis draws from the attribute of Omnipotence using the same structure I used at the beginning of the chapter to examine the beliefs taught by Augustine,

Luther, Calvin, and Sproul on Omniscience, Omnipotence, and Perfection:

C. S. Lewis reads in scripture that God is Omnipotent. In Genesis God gave man the freedom to eat from any tree. This means that man was free to eat from any tree, and God could not prevent the opportunity for man to do so. If God prevented man from sinning then God did what is logically contradictory: He gave man freedom and withheld it from man at the same time and in the same sense. The fall of Lucifer and the fall of man was not God's will, it was done against God's will, and it is not that His power met an immovable object, it is that Lucifer and man abused the power that He gave to them. God ordained that Lucifer and man were "free" but they were not "free" from His sovereign rule. God did not "ordain" that Lucifer or man sin. The following are several quotes from C. S. Lewis regarding the fall:

C. S. Lewis discusses this view of the fall and free-will in man:

(Lewis:) "God created things which had free-will. That means creatures which can go either wrong or right. Some people think they can imagine a creature which was free but had no possibility of going wrong; I cannot. If a thing is free to be good it is also free to be bad. And free-will is what has made evil possible. Why, then, did God give them free-will? Because free-will, though it makes evil possible, is also the only thing that makes possible any love or goodness or joy worth having. A world of automata -- of creatures that worked like machines -- would hardly be worth creating. The happiness which God designs for His higher creatures is the happiness of being freely, voluntarily united to Him and to each other in an ecstasy of love and delight compared with which the most rapturous love between a man and a woman on this earth is mere milk and water. And for that they must be free."

"Of course God knew what would happen if they used their freedom the wrong way: apparently He thought it worth the risk. Perhaps we feel inclined to disagree with Him. But there is a difficulty about disagreeing with God. He is the source from which all your reasoning power comes: you could not be right and He wrong any more than a stream can rise higher than its own source. When you are arguing against Him you are arguing against the very power that makes you able to argue at all: it is like cutting off the branch you are sitting on. If God thinks this state of war in the universe a price worth paying for free-will -- that is, for making a live world in which creatures can do real good or harm and something of real importance can happen, instead of a toy world which only moves when He pulls the strings -- then we may take it, it is worth paying." (MC, p. 34)

C. S. Lewis discusses the notion that God could prevent the fall:

(Lewis:) "We can, perhaps, conceive of a world in which God corrected the results of this abuse of free-will by His creatures at every moment: so that a wooden beam became soft as grass when it was used as a weapon, and the air refused to obey me if I attempted to set up in it the sound-waves that carry lies or insults. But such a world would be one in which wrong actions were impossible, and in which, therefore, freedom of the will would be void; nay, if the principle were carried out to its logical conclusion, evil thoughts would be impossible, for the cerebral matter which we use in thinking would refuse its task when we attempted to frame them." (POP, p. 382)

At this point, we need to discuss "free-will". What I understand C. S. Lewis to be saying here is that God made man responsible for the choices man would make. Norman Geisler gives us the definition of responsibility: "the ability to respond one way or another." (CBF, p. 30) This fits with Genesis 2: 16 - 17, that man was given the ability to eat, or not eat, from the tree of the knowledge of good and evil. Man was not given "autonomy" (meaning self-law), Adam was still under the rule of God. "Free-will" then means: free from coercion, both external and internal, but not free from persuasion or influences, both external and internal in the decisions for which man is responsible. God was not passive: He gave man the ability not to sin, and the instruction not to sin.
Geisler explains how this view of free-will in man makes man responsible for the fall:

(Geisler:) "*Adam and Eve's* free will *was* not the efficient cause of *their* free act; it *was* simply the power through which *they performed* the free act. *Their actions came about by the means of their will.* The efficient cause of a free act is really the free agent, not the free choice. Free choice is simply the power by which the free agent acts. We do not say that a person is free choice but simply that the person has free choice. Likewise, we do not say man is thought but only that he has the power of thought. So it is not the power of free choice that causes a free act, but

41

the <u>person</u> who has this power." (CBF, Appendix four - words in italics are my addition - underline is of words italicized in original).

To a certain extent, Calvin agrees with Geisler's explanation:

(Calvin:) I have everywhere asserted, that man was created, in the beginning, perfectly upright. (EPG, p. 112)   Adam fell by the instigation of the Devil, and by the impulse of his own heart. (EPG, p. 112)

R.C. Sproul gives a definition of free-will that is used against those that do not agree with Reformed Theology:

(Sproul:) Probably the most common definition says *free-will is the ability to make choices without any prior prejudice, inclination, or disposition.* For the will to be free it must act from a posture of neutrality, with absolutely no bias. (CBG, p. 51 - italics in original)

It is easy to see why Calvinists and non-Calvinists speak past each other. Neither Calvinists or non-Calvinists would agree with the definition of free-will Sproul gives. Non-Calvinists do not need lengthy explanations from Jonathan Edwards on how this definition does not make any sense since they already agree that it is nonsense. Adam was not free from God commanding him to not eat from the tree of the knowledge of good and evil. Eve received the instruction from Adam. Neither were they free from the tempting by the serpent. Their will was not neutral, "*without any prior prejudice, inclination, or disposition.*" "Free-will" means that their choice was not coerced. God could not coerce them to not eat the forbidden fruit, and Satan could not simply overpower Adam -- jamming the fruit into his mouth and forcing him to chew and swallow. The act had to be voluntary for Adam and Eve to be held responsible. To be responsible, they had to have the ability to respond one way or the other.

Calvin admits that Adam being held responsible when Adam had to sin since God willed Adam to sin, ordained Adam to sin, and decreed that Adam would sin, is a problem in Reformed Theology.

(Calvin:) "But it could not be otherwise, <u>Adam could not but fall</u>; <u>according to the foreknowledge</u>, <u>and will of God</u>. What then! - - <u>is</u> <u>Adam</u>, <u>on that account</u>, <u>freed from fault</u>? <u>Certainly not</u>. He fell by his own full free-will; and by his own willing act." (EPG, p. 76)

R. C. Sproul explains the problem Calvinists are faced with since they begin the assumption that God could have prevented the fall of both Lucifer and Adam, and they have a "straw man" definition of free-will:

(Sproul:) "Again we hear the 'easy' explanation that evil came through the creature's free-will. Free-will is a good thing. That God gave us free-will does not cast blame on Him. In creation man was given an ability to sin and an ability not to sin. He chose to sin. The question is, 'Why?' " (CBG, p. 30 - Excuse the reminder that Sproul answers his own question by saying that God foreordained man to sin and decreed that man would sin. The 'easy' explanation that evil came through Adam's free-will negates the Reformed view that God willed, ordained, and decreed the fall to happen -- which is not 'easy' to explain.)

R. C. Sproul continues:

(Sproul:) "Herein lies the problem. Before a person can commit an act of sin he must first have a desire to perform that act. The Bible tells us that evil actions flow from evil desires. But the presence of an evil desire is already sin. We sin because we are sinners. We were born with a sin nature. We are fallen creatures. But Adam and Eve were not created fallen. They had no sin nature. They were good creatures with a free-will. Yet they chose to sin. Why? I don't know. Nor have I found anyone yet who does know. " (CBG, pp. 30 - 31 Note: Calvin tells us why: It was God's will that Adam and Eve sin. The correct question is not "why" Adam and Eve sinned, but "how?": Did they sin with the ordaining will of God, or by their own free-will and against the will of God?)
"In spite of this excruciating problem we still must affirm that God is not the author of sin. The Bible does not reveal the answers to all our questions. It does reveal the nature and character of God. One thing is absolutely unthinkable, that God could be the author or doer of sin." (CBG, p. 31)

This is how Calvin dealt with the "excruciating problem" that God ordaining Adam and Eve to sin and fall leads to the logical conclusion that God is the Author of evil and doer of sin:

(Calvin:) "That the eternal predestination of God, by which He decreed, before the Fall of Adam, what should take place, in the whole human race, and in every individual thereof, was unalterably fixed and determined." (EPG, p. 108) "Adam fell not, nor destroyed himself and his posterity, either *without* the knowledge, or *without* the ordaining will of God, yet *that* neither lessens his own fault, nor implicates God in any blame whatever." (EPG, p. 109 - underline is mine - italics in original)

(Calvin:) "Wherefore, in ordaining the Fall of man, especially, God had an end most glorious and most just; an end, into our contemplation of which, the mention or idea, of *sin* on the part of God, can never enter; the very *thought* of its entrance, strikes us with horror! Although, therefore, I thus affirm that God did ordain the Fall of Adam, I so assert it, as by no means to concede, that God was therein, properly and really, the author of that Fall. I will only express it, as my view, belief, and sentiment, that what Augustine so deeply teaches, on this matter, was *fulfilled* in God's ordaining the Fall of Adam: "In a wonderful and unutterable way, *that* was not done *without* the will of God (says he), which was even done *contrary* to His will; *because*, it could not have been done at all, if His will had not *permitted* it to be done. And yet, He did not permit it *unwillingly*, but *willingly*." The great and grand principle, therefore, on which Augustine argues cannot be denied: "That, both man, and apostate angels, as far as they were themselves concerned, did *that* which God *willed not*, or which was *contrary to* HIS WILL; but that, as far as God's overruling Omnipotence is concerned, they could not, in any manner, have done it, *without* His will." To these sentiments of the holy man I subscribe, with all my heart." (EPG, p. 111 - underline is mine - italics in original)

(Calvin:) "So far, however, am I from undertaking to explain this sublime and hidden mystery, by any powers of human reason, that I would ever retain in my own memory, that which I declared, at the commencement of this discussion: that those who seek to know more than God has revealed are *madmen*! Wherefore, let us delight ourselves more in wise ignorance, than in an immoderate and intoxicated curiosity to know more than God permits." (EPG, pp. 111 - 112 - italics in original)

(Calvin:) "But *HOW* it was, that God, by His foreknowledge and decree, ordained what should take place in Adam, and yet, so ordained it, without His being Himself, in the least, a participator of the fault, or being at all the author or the approver of the transgression; *how* this was, I repeat, is a secret, manifestly far too deep to be penetrated by any stretch of human intellect. Herein, therefore, I am not ashamed to confess my utter ignorance." (EPG, pp. 112 - 113 - Underline is mine - italics in original - As pointed out above, Sproul asks "Why?" while Calvin correctly asks "How?")

This quote from G. K. Chesterton sums it up nicely:

(Chesterton:) "Only a man who knows nothing of motors talks of motoring without petrol; only a man who knows nothing of reason talks of reasoning without strong, undisputed first principles." (BC, p. 20)

The difference between the first principles of Calvin and C. S. Lewis should be clear at this point. C. S. Lewis is saying that the Calvinistic view is built upon a false assumption and a logically contradictory view of the Omnipotence of God. C. S. Lewis is not saying that Calvinism is wrong because it makes God the author of evil, even though it does that too. C. S. Lewis is saying that first and foremost, Calvinism is built upon a logical contradiction.

This foundational, logically contradictory belief, leads to the conclusion that it must be God's will that man and angels fell. This belief leads to the conclusion that God is the Author of evil, which "strikes us with horror!" The solution to this logical contradiction of God willing that man and angels sin, and God not willing that man and angels should sin, is resolved by Calvinists in their view of the attribute of Omni-benevolence in God.

CHAPTER FOUR

The very first assumption of Calvinism is that God is free to over-rule any of His creatures' decisions, so God could have prevented Adam from sinning; Therefore, God must have willed the fall to happen. Since we cannot reason how it is good that man sin, we do not know what good is. Whatever God wills is good: God willed the fall to happen, since the fall happened and the fall could not have happened if He did not will it to happen.

Whatever God wills is good: The fall must be good since He willed it, and since man cannot understand how the fall is good, man does not know what good is. In fact, man has such a distorted view of good that it even appears to man that God ordaining and willing the fall to happen makes God the author of evil, and there is no evil in a perfect, righteous God. The obvious solution is that what God wills is therefore right because He wills it, and His will is higher than reason.

Foundation of Reformed Theology / Calvinism:
1. God is free to over-rule any of His creatures' decisions.
2.   A. God is Omniscient
       B. God is Omnipotent
       C. God is Perfect
3.   A. God knew the fall would happen.
       B. God could have stopped the fall from happening.
       C. God did not need to create anything.
4. The fall was willed, ordained, and decreed by God > Everything that happens is the will of God.
5. No free-will in man or angel.
6. Correct because God wills it > Created for the Glory of God.
7. Man does not know what good is.
8. Total Depravity or Total Inability > Three meanings of Faith

----

The answer to the problem of a Omni-benevolent God ordaining evil to happen is a philosophical system called "voluntarism". Philosophical Voluntarism is the theory that God is to be conceived of as some form of will. The question that is being asked is: "Is something correct, therefore God wills it", or "Does God will something, therefore it is correct". Calvinism agrees with the latter: God wills something, therefore it is correct.

Voluntarism: God has a will, whatever He wills is correct, because He willed it.

The following quote by Martin Luther <u>describes God as some form of will</u> and teaches that <u>God wills something</u>, <u>therefore it is correct</u>:

(Luther:) "God is that Being for <u>whose will no cause or reason is to be assigned</u>, as a rule or standard by which it acts." and "What God wills, is not therefore right, because He ought or ever was bound so to will; but on the contrary, <u>what takes place is therefore right</u>, <u>because He so wills</u>." (On the Bondage of the Will, pp. 230 - 231 - underline is mine)

When Luther couples omnipotence, omniscience, and voluntarism, he gives us the following statement about the Will of God and the possibility of "Free-will" in both man and angels:

(Luther:) For if we believe it to be true, that God fore-knows and fore-ordains all things; that He can be neither deceived nor hindered in His Prescience and predestination; and that nothing can take place but according to His Will, (which reason herself is compelled to confess;) then, even according to the testimony of reason herself, there can be no "Free-will" --in man, --in angel, --or in any creature! (The Bondage of the Will, p. 390 - underline is mine)

The following quotes from Calvin show the primacy of the will over reason in the Omni-benevolence of God, showing that Calvin agrees with Luther and Voluntarism:

(Calvin:) "Why does Paul so particularly say, that the children had done neither good nor evil? But, that he might do away with all respect of merit in them? Why? But that he might positively affirm, that <u>God drew His reasons from no other source,</u> <u>than from His own mind and will,</u> when He pronounced so different a judgment on the twin brothers?" (EPG, pp. 43 - 44 - underline is mine)

(Calvin:) "Yet, God had, at the first, in His conversation with Moses, claimed to Himself the free right of exercising His mercy as, and towards whom, He pleased. And this He did, <u>that no one might dare to prescribe a law for *His* actions</u>." (EPG, pp. 47 - 48 - underline is mine - italics in

47

original)

(Calvin:) "And that no law can be imposed on Him as a rule for His works: *because* no law or rule can be thought of, better, greater, or more just, than His own will!" (EPG, p. 51 - italics in original)

(Calvin:) "Whenever therefore, <u>we carry the *will* of God to its utmost height, and show that it is *higher than* all reason,</u> far be it from us to imagine, that He ever *wills* anything but *with* the *highest reason*." (EPG, p. 103 - underline is mine - italics in original)

(Calvin:) "It is therefore our duty to rest in His will alone. So that our knowledge of His *will* and *pleasure*, in whatsoever He doeth, though the cause of His doing it should surpass our comprehension, ought to suffice us, more than a thousand reasons." (EPG, p. 106 - italics in original)

(Calvin:) "But what *knowledge* of *the cause* can I be said to profess, if I only believe, that God does, what He does, with a great design, and what He judges right to be done: and especially, if <u>I profess myself to be, all the while, unable to *comprehend* the certain and special *reason* of the Divine work and counsel</u>?" (EPG, p. 106 - italics in original - underline is mine)

After explaining that he is unable to comprehend the Divine work and counsel, Calvin explains the destruction of any free-will in fallen man and gives the definition of Total Depravity: Man is utterly incapable of understanding the things of God.

(Calvin:) "What is *free-will*? when the Scripture everywhere declares, that man, being the captive, the servant, and the slave of the devil, is carried away into wickedness of every kind, with his *whole mind* and *inclination*; <u>being utterly incapable of *understanding* the things of God, much less of *doing* them</u>?" (EPG, p. 192 - underline is mine - italics in original)

In Calvinism, whatever God wills is correct, and nothing can happen except God wills it. As the quote from Luther just explained: Everything that happens is the will of God. God must "ordain" evil to happen, or it could not be here. Since evil exists, God willed (decreed or ordained) it to happen. God willed evil to happen, and God continues to will that evil happens.

Calvin agrees with Luther that everything that happens is the will of God:

(Calvin:) "Nothing, therefore, is done, but that which the Omnipotent *willed* to be done, either by permitting it to be done, or by doing it Himself." (EPG, p. 25 - italics in original)

R.C. Sproul agrees with this and states the problem Calvinists face:

(Sproul:) "Then, as now, I realized that evil was a problem for the sovereignty of God. Did evil come into the world against God's sovereign will? If so, then He is not absolutely sovereign. If not, then we must conclude that in some sense even evil is foreordained by God." (CBG, p. 29)

(Sproul:) "We know that God is sovereign because we know that God is God. Therefore we must conclude that God foreordained sin. What else can we conclude?" (CBG, p. 31)

Albert Mohler will explain how we need to look through the philosophical glasses of voluntarism to see that God ordaining and willing evil to happen is good. Since we are unable to comprehend the Divine, and we are utterly incapable of understanding the will or mind of God, we do not know what good is. We cannot use reason to know what "good" is for God, since His will is above reason. ("Theodicy" is an attempt to reconcile God with the existence of evil.) :

(Mohler:) "I think there are two other very important issues here. The entire problem with theodicy arises from a wrong question or a wrong presumption, in other words, rather than seeing God as essentially good, and deriving whatever good is from observing the one true and living God, we abstract an idea of good, and then try to measure God against that human abstraction. That is always a losing proposition, because we don't know what good is, that's the problem, when persons come up to us and say if God does this He cannot be good, they don't realize that is an internal contradiction. The only God that exists is a God who is good, He defines what is good by consistency in His own character. Not by the fact that He corresponds to some arbitrary understanding of good. We have to have an eschatological perspective on this always, and I have this absolute confidence, and I want to cite James Montgomery Boice, God's judgment in the end will be so absolutely perfect that the damned will agree with the rightness of their damnation. There will be no question at that point, that evil will be seen for the evil it was, but God's goodness will be demonstrated for the goodness that is. We are really dependent on the eyes of faith to see this, but we must never fall into the trap, we can't accept the presumption that we are trying to defend God over against a human abstraction called good. Instead we simply have to come back, again and again, to the fact that God is good, whatever He does is good, His will is consistent with His character." (National Conference, 2007 - underline is mine)

Calvinism and Voluntarism does not just argue against "some arbitrary understanding of good," it argues against a "Natural Law," which is a way for man to know what is good. As Calvin stated, "that no one might dare to prescribe a law for His actions", which is what a Natural Law would do. Mohler says "that God is good, whatever He does is good," since everything that happens is the will of God, God willing that evil take place is good, since He will bring good out of it. Once again this is consistent with Calvin and Augustine:

(Calvin:) "He also knew, that it was more to the glory of His omnipotent goodness, to bring good out of evil, than not to permit evil to be at all!" (EPG, p. 25)

The Calvinist view of Omnipotence, leads to the voluntarist view of the Omni-benevolence of God, which teaches that we do not know what good is. Voluntarism leads to the doctrine of Total Inability and Total Depravity, that because we do not know what good is, we are unable to do good, and unable to believe in God:

(Five Points:) "Because of the fall, man is unable of himself to savingly believe the gospel. The sinner is dead, blind, and deaf to the things of God; his heart is deceitful and desperately corrupt. His will is not free, it is in bondage to his evil nature, therefore, he will not -- indeed he cannot -- choose good over evil in the spiritual realm. Consequently, it takes much more than the Spirit's assistance to bring a sinner to Christ -- it takes regeneration by which the Spirit makes the sinner alive and gives him a new nature. Faith is not something man contributes to salvation but is itself a part of God's gift to the sinner, not the sinner's gift to God." (Five Points, p. 16 - underline is mine)

Calvinists disagree with the following statement by C. S. Lewis:

(Lewis:) "There are only two kinds of people in the end: those who say to God, 'Thy will be done,' and those to whom God says, in the end, '*Thy will be done*'." (TGD, p. 340 - italics in original)

Calvinists would say that C. S. Lewis is incorrect, because everything that happens is the will of God. It is God's will that the elect go to heaven and it is God's will that the reprobate go to hell. Who would be so silly as the say that God is not sovereign over who goes to heaven and who goes to hell? If this seems unfair to you, it is because you "don't know what good is." You are projecting your sense of justice upon God. God wills evil to happen so that He can bring good out of it. "The only God that exists is a God who is good." While God wills evil to happen, since God is good, evil will be seen as good when we look back on it from eternity. If you do not understand how God ordaining that you do evil is good, or that someone else doing evil to you is good, it is because you are "utterly incapable of understanding the things of God" and you "don't know what good is." The following verse and its interpretation by Calvinists illustrates the application of this system of belief:

"But Joseph said to them, 'Do not fear, for am I in the place of God? As for you, you meant evil against me, but God meant it for good, to bring it about that many people should be kept alive, as they are today'." Genesis 50:19 - 20 (ESV)

James White states that: "Joseph well knew the motivations of his brothers when they sold him into slavery. But, in the very same event he saw the over-riding hand of God, guiding, directing, and ultimately meaning *in the same action* to bring about good." White agrees that "God decreed that this event would take place." (PF, p. 48 - italics in original) In Reformed theology, God has a decreeing will, an ordaining will, a desiring will, a permissive will, a secret will, etc.

"The word which came to Jeremiah from the LORD, saying, Arise, and go down to the potter's house, and there I will cause thee to hear my words. Then I went down to the potter's house, and, behold, he wrought a work on the wheels. And <u>the vessel that he made of clay was marred in the hand of the potter</u>: so he made it again another vessel, as seemed good to the potter to make it." Jeremiah 18:1 - 4 (ESV - underline is mine)

From Calvin's commentary on Jeremiah 18: "The Prophet was commanded to go down to the potter's house, that he might relate to the people what he saw there, even that <u>the potter, according to his own will and pleasure, made and re-made vessels</u>." "As the clay is at the will and under the power of the potter, so men are at the will of God: God then is compared to the potter." "God determined, before the creation of the world, what he pleased respecting each individual."

In Calvinism, God willed that the fall should happen. It was God's will that Adam sin and become marred so that God could make Adam, and all of Adam's posterity, over into whatever it pleases Him to make. God deliberately marred the vessel of clay that was in His hands in order that He might make it over again as He sees fit. Adam did not mar himself against the over-ruling Omnipotent will of God. Instead, Adam marred himself in accord with the permissive will, and the over-ruling Omnipotent will, of God.

Here is a lengthy quote from Calvin saying this exact thing, that the vessels in Jeremiah 18 are deliberately made that way by God, not by their own actions:

(Calvin:) "Now if this being "*afore prepared* unto glory" is peculiar and special to the elect; it evidently follows, that the rest, <u>the non-elect, were equally "*fitted* to destruction</u>:" because, being left to their own nature, they were thereby devoted already to certain destruction. <u>That they were "fitted to destruction" by *their own wickedness*, is an idea so silly, that it needs no notice</u>. It is indeed true, that the reprobate procure to themselves the wrath of God; and that they daily hasten on the falling of its weight upon their own heads. But it must be confessed by all, that <u>the apostle is here treating of that difference made between the elect and the reprobate, which proceeds from the alone secret will and purpose of God</u>." (EPG, p. 60 - italics in original - underline is mine)

Now that we have summarized the Calvinist position, I will review how C. S. Lewis gets to this same point and has a different view on the Omni-benevolence of God. The beginning assumption for C. S. Lewis is that it is logically contradictory to say that God could have prevented man or Lucifer from sinning. It was God's will to give Lucifer and man free-will, but their use of it went against His will, and it is logically contradictory to say that God can give man free-will and withhold it at the same time.

Foundation of Classical Theism:
1. God is free to give freedom to His creatures.
2.   A. God is Omniscient
       B. God is Omnipotent
       C. God is Perfect
3.   A. God knew the fall would happen.
       B. God could not stop the fall from happening.
       C. God did not need to create anything.
4. The fall was not ordained by God > God chose to give man the ability to choose.
5. Man and Angels are "Free Moral Agents".
6. Something is Correct; Therefore, God wills it. > Man created so God could Love us.
7. The ability for man to know good and evil is impaired.
8. Unrighteous with impaired ability > Faith - ability to believe - common to all.

C. S. Lewis discusses whether or not we can know what good is:

(Lewis:) "Any consideration of the goodness of God at once threatens us with the following dilemma.

On the one hand, if God is wiser than we His judgment must differ from ours on many things, and not least on good and evil. What seems to us good may therefore not be good in His eyes, and what seems to us evil may not be evil.

On the other hand, if God's moral judgment differs from ours so that our 'black' may be His 'white', we can mean nothing by calling Him good; for to say 'God is good', while asserting that His goodness is wholly other than ours, is really only to say 'God is we know not what'. And an utterly unknown quality in God cannot give us moral ground for loving or obeying Him. If He is not (in our sense) 'good' we shall obey, if at all, only through fear -- and should be equally ready to obey an omnipotent Fiend. The doctrine of Total Depravity -- when the consequence is drawn that, since we are totally depraved, our idea of good is worth simply nothing -- may thus turn Christianity into a form of devil-worship." (POP, 384 - underline is mine)

C. S. Lewis explains how we know what good is, but not perfectly. We have an impaired ability to know what good is:

(Lewis:) "The Divine 'goodness' differs from ours, but it is not sheerly different: it differs from ours not as white from black but as a perfect circle from a child's first attempt to draw a wheel. But when the child has learned to draw, it will know that the circle it then makes is what it was trying to make from the very beginning."
"This doctrine is presupposed in Scripture. Christ calls men to repent -- a call which would be meaningless if God's standards were sheerly different from that which they already knew and failed to practice. He appeals to our existing moral judgment -- 'Why even of yourselves judge ye not what is right?' (Luke 12:57) God in the Old Testament expostulates with men on the basis of their own conceptions of gratitude, fidelity, and fair play: and puts Himself, as it were, at the bar before His own creatures -- 'What iniquity have your fathers found in me, that they are gone far from me?' " (Jeremiah 2:5) (POP, p. 385: See Acts 17:30 for call to repent)

C. S. Lewis explains that he believes something is good; therefore, God wills it. That there is an intrinsic right and wrong, or natural law. He also points out the logical conclusion of voluntarism:

(Lewis:) "It has sometimes been asked whether God commands certain things because they are right, or whether certain things are right because God commands them. With Hooker, and against Dr Johnson, I emphatically embrace the first alternative. The second might lead to the abominable conclusion (reached, I think, by Paley) that charity is good only because God arbitrarily commanded it -- that He might equally well have commanded us to hate Him and one another and that hatred would then have been right. I believe, on the contrary, that 'they err who think that of the will of God to do this or that there is no reason besides His will'. (Hooker, Laws of Eccl. Polity, I, I, 5.) God's will is determined by His wisdom which always perceives, and His goodness which always embraces, the intrinsically good." (POP, p. 409)

Both Calvin and C. S. Lewis have to answer the same question: Is something correct, therefore God wills it, or: Does God will something, therefore it is correct. Calvin takes the second option and voluntarism. C. S. Lewis takes the first option and what is called "intellectualism." The quickest way to decide if voluntarism is correct, is to compare its logical conclusion to scripture. Remember Albert Mohler saying, "We don't know what good is." God the Father has something to say about this:

"Then the LORD God said, "Behold, <u>the man has become like one of Us in knowing good and evil</u>. Now, lest he reach out his hand and take also of the tree of life and eat, and live forever--" therefore the LORD God sent him out from the garden of Eden to work the ground from which he was taken." Genesis 3:22 - 23 (ESV - Underline is mine)

God tells us in Scripture that we have become like Him in our ability to know good from evil.

Calvin tells us that man is utterly incapable of understanding the things of God.

Mohler tells us that man does not know what good is.

Scripture tells us that both man and God have the ability to know good and evil.

If we agree with Calvin and Mohler that man does not know what good is, and we agree with Scripture that man and God have a similar ability to know what good is, then we arrive at the absurd conclusion that both man and God do not know what good is.

This simple comparison of Reformed Theology and voluntarism with Scripture should be adequate to show that they are in error.

In contrast to voluntarism, intellectualism believes that there is an intrinsic good and evil. That there is a reason for what God wills. For example, Love is intrinsically good since it carries its goodness within itself:

55

"Love is patient and kind; love does not envy or boast; it is not arrogant or rude. It does not insist on its own way; it is not irritable or resentful; it does not rejoice at wrongdoing, but rejoices with the truth. Love bears all things, believes all things, hopes all things, endures all things. Love never ends. As for prophecies, they will pass away; as for tongues, they will cease; as for knowledge, it will pass away." 1 Corinthians 13:4 - 8 (ESV)

Just as Love is intrinsically good, sin is intrinsically evil:

"For you are not a God who delights in wickedness; evil may not dwell with you. The boastful shall not stand before your eyes; you hate all evildoers." Psalms 5:4 - 5 (ESV)

While sin and evil carry their "not goodness" intrinsically, hate does not. If I hate a person simply because of the color of their skin, I do evil. If I hate evil, I do good.

"Seek good, and not evil, that you may live; and so the LORD, the God of hosts, will be with you, as you have said. Hate evil, and love good, and establish justice in the gate; it may be that the LORD, the God of hosts, will be gracious to the remnant of Joseph." Amos 5:14 - 15 (ESV)

Remember this quote from Chapter Two: "This does not make God subject to something beyond Himself. When God is subject to good reason (logic), He is subject to His own nature, since He is the ultimate Reason or Logos (John 1:1). Likewise, when God is subject to the law of justice, He is not bound by something beyond Himself, but to something within Himself, which is His own unchangeable nature." (ST 1, p. 91)

(Lewis:) (This "natural law") "...is the doctrine of objective value, the belief that certain attitudes are really true, and others really false, to the kind of thing the universe is and the kind of things we are." (Abolition, p. 473 - words in parentheses are mine)

G. K. Chesterton also gives a description of the intrinsically good:

(Chesterton:) "Reason and justice grip the remotest and the loneliest star. Look at those stars. Don't they look as if they were single diamonds and sapphires? Well, you can imagine any mad botany or geology you please. Think of forest of adamant with leaves of brilliants. Think the moon is a blue moon, a single elephantine sapphire. But don't fancy that all that frantic astronomy would make the smallest difference to the reason and justice of conduct. On plains of opal, under cliffs cut out of pearl, you would still find a notice board, "Thou shalt not steal." " (BC, p. 29)

Instead of not being able to know what good is, our ability to know good has been impaired. Just as Lucifer's judgment was impaired by pride, and Adam's judgment was impaired by the tempting of the serpent.

Geisler explains how we know what good is; However, since our ability is impaired, we do not know perfectly what good is:

(Geisler:) "Another clue to understanding natural revelation is our basic moral *inclinations*. This is why our best understanding of the natural law comes not from seeing our actions but from observing our reactions: *We know the moral law instinctively*. We don't have to read it in any book; we know it intuitively, written as it is on our own heart. So when interpreting the natural law, we must be careful to do so from reactions truly indicative of it. These are not necessarily the ones we *do to others*, but more often those that we *desire to be done to us*. Once again, Paul speaks to this point when he writes of the things we "do by nature" that "show" the moral law "written on our hearts" " (Romans 2:14 - 15).

(Geisler:) "Our moral inclinations are manifested in our reactions when others violate *our* rights; we don't see the moral law nearly as clearly when we violate *others'* rights. Herein is revealed our depravity. But again our sinfulness is not found in our inability to know what the moral duty is but in our unwillingness to do it to others.
"The kind of reactions that manifest the natural moral law were brought home forcefully to me when a professor, after carefully reading a student's well-researched paper defending moral relativity, wrote: " F. *I do not like blue folders*." After receiving his grade, the student stormed into his professor's office, protesting, "That's not fair. That's not just!" The student's reaction to the injustice done to him revealed, contrary to what he wrote, that deep down inside he really did believe in an objective

moral principle of rightness. The real measure of his morals was not what he had written in his paper but what God had written on his heart. What he really believed was right manifested itself when he was wronged." (ST 1, pp. 75 - 76 - italics in original)

In *Chosen by God*, on page 14, R. C. Sproul has a table listing Saint Thomas Aquinas as teaching the "Reformed" view. Aquinas systematized what is called Classical Theism, the belief that God is absolutely simple in His essence while His creatures are composed. Sproul uses Classical Theism to explain the reformed view of how God's attribute of Love relates to God's attribute of sovereignty:

(Sproul:) "When we consider love as an attribute of God, we recognize that it is defined in relation to all the other attributes of God. This is true not only of love but also of every other attribute of God. It is important to remember that when we speak of the attributes of God, we are speaking of properties that cannot be reduced to composite parts. One of the first affirmations we make about the nature of God is that He is not a composite being. Rather we confess that God is a simple being. This does not mean that God is 'easy' in the sense that a simple task is not a difficult task. Here simplicity is not contrasted with difficulty but with composition. A being who is composite is made up of definite parts. As a human creature, I am composed of many parts, such as arms, legs, eyes, ears, lungs, etc."
"As a simple being, God is not made up of parts as we are. This is crucial to any proper understanding of the nature of God. This means that God is not partly immutable, partly omniscient, partly omnipotent, or partly infinite. He is not constructed of a section or segment of being that is then added to other sections or segments to comprise the whole of God. It is not so much that God *has* attributes but rather that He *is* His attributes. In simple terms (as distinct from difficult terms) this means that all of God's attributes help define all of His other attributes. For example, when we say God is immutable, we are also saying that His immutability is an eternal immutability, an omnipotent immutability, a holy immutability, a loving immutability, etc. By the same token His love is an immutable love, an eternal love, an omnipotent love, a holy love, etc." (Loved, pp. 6 - 7 - underline is mine - italics in original)

58

Up to this point, Sproul has accurately represented what Aquinas systematized in his *Summa Theologica*. This philosophical system is called "Classical Theism" and in its most basic form states that God is absolutely simple (meaning "indivisible"), while all of the creatures He created are composed (meaning they have "potentiality," which is the ability to change or the possibility of change).

An absolutely simple God cannot change, He is "immutable". God is already perfect, He cannot become more perfect. God is omniscient, He cannot become more knowing. The attributes of God are "extensive", meaning that each attribute extends to every other attribute. God knows how to love perfectly and is able to do so. Here is the same sentence with each attribute in parentheses: God knows (Omniscience) how to love (Love) perfectly (Perfection) and is able (Omnipotence) to do so. His Love never changes (immutable). Aquinas, Sproul, and C. S. Lewis agree on this view of God.

God differs from His creation which has potentiality. A tree grows and changes. The tree can be cut down and made into a table. Reading this book has changed you. You have grown older and learned something. The angels learned from the fall of Lucifer and one third of the angels. Understanding this difference shows the importance of discovering and carefully defining what the attributes of God are.

R. C. Sproul continues on and explains how Calvinists consider sovereignty to be an attribute of God that is part of the simple, indivisible, essence of God:

(Sproul:) "The need to be vigilant with respect to our natural instincts toward idolatry is especially acute when we are considering the love of God. I doubt there is another attribute of God more fraught with the peril of idolatry than this one. It is the attribute most often selected at our theological smorgasbord.
When lecturing on the holiness of God, the sovereignty of God, the justice of God, or the wrath of God, many times I am interrupted by someone who comments, "But my God is a God of love." I hasten to assure the person that I also believe in a God of love. But I often note in the protest a thinly veiled suggestion that the love of God is somehow incompatible with his holiness, justice, <u>sovereignty</u>, or wrath. <u>Here the attribute of love has been isolated from God's other attributes</u> so that it is the only attribute by which God is known or it subsumes or swallows up all of His other attributes.

This is precisely what happens when we conceive of God as a composite being rather than a simple one. We have a structure that allows us to pick and choose our attributes and gives us a license to construct a god who is an idol. If the Bible is our primary source for God's revelation of His nature and character and it declares that God is holy, just, <u>sovereign</u>, and wrathful, as well as loving, then <u>we need to understand the love of God in such a way that it does not negate or swallow up these other attributes</u>." (Loved, pp. 8 - 9 - underline is mine)

(Sproul:) "<u>This reveals that behind or along with the electing love of God stands His sovereignty</u>. We see that not only is God's will sovereign but <u>His love is also sovereign</u>." (Loved, p. 89 - underline is mine)

The conclusion is easily reached that God is sovereign over His love, which explains why God could Love Jacob and Hate Esau before the twins had done either good or evil. Sproul agrees with Aquinas that "Love" is an attribute of God. Aquinas agrees with Sproul that God is sovereign. The difference between Calvinists and Classical Theists is how God is sovereign:

The following explanation is from Geisler's Systematic Theology, which will explain how the two views differ from each other:

(Geisler:) "How many attributes does God have?
Different theologians list different numbers. This is (1) partly due to the fact that some theologians are not attempting to give a comprehensive list; (2) partly because some theologians combine certain attributes into one; (3) partly owing to the disagreement as to whether some attributes are really attributes or whether that are *activities* of God (e.g. mercy); and (4) <u>partly because some theologians do not distinguish between an attribute</u> (which is of <u>God's essence</u>, such as holiness) <u>and a characteristic</u> (which is not an attribute but is simply something that belongs to God in general, such as ineffability).
Other Nonmoral Characteristics of God
<u>These involve how God, in His essential attributes, relates to His creatures</u>. They include <u>sovereignty</u>, transcendence, immanence, omnipresence, and ineffability. <u>Without a creation, God would have nothing to be sovereign over</u>, transcendent above, immanent in, or omnipresent to. <u>God's essential attributes, however, are proper to His</u>

nature as such, <u>even if there were no creatures with whom/which to relate</u>." (ST 2, p. 20 - 21 - underline is mine - italics in original)

R. C. Sproul is saying that sovereignty and love are in the essence of God, which means that these two attributes *extend* to each other. God will be sovereign in a loving way <u>and</u> God is sovereign over His love.

Geisler is saying that sovereignty is not *extensive* with God's attribute of love because it is not an essential attribute of God. Sovereignty flows from the essence of God: God is sovereign because He is all-powerful, all-good, all-knowing, and all-wise. Classical Theists agree with scripture that God does whatever He pleases, but it pleases God to be sovereign in a way that is consistent with His nature. Classical Theists agree with Calvinists that Nature is over Will in man. Classical Theists also believe that the Nature of God is over the Will of God, or that the will of God flows from His nature or essence.

God could not will that evil happen since God is Light and there is no darkness in Him. (1 John 1:5)

Contrary to Classical Theism, Voluntarism teaches that God is to be conceived of as some form of will. This view may place the will of God over the nature of God, or it makes the will of God identical with the nature of God (instead of the nature of God being over the will of God, or the will of God flowing from His nature or essence).

In *Summa Theologica*, Aquinas does put "providence" in the essence of God. Providence is the means by which God is in control over all, while sovereignty is God's right to control all things. Providence, the means by which God is in control, is by His attributes of Omnipotence, Omni-benevolence, Omniscience, Wisdom, and Omnipresence. These attributes are proper to the nature of God and are in His essence. God is Sovereign because He has the right to use these attributes. Sovereignty flows from His essential attributes, and is a characteristic of God that is attributed to Him, it is not an attribute itself. I believe that this misunderstanding by Sproul is why he incorrectly lists Aquinas as being Reformed.

The reformed view of the Omnipotence of God in relation to the fall, drives all Calvinists to a Voluntaristic view of the Omni-benevolence of God. Reformed theology agrees with John Duns Scotus on the attribute of Omnipotence. Scotus taught that the attributes of God were to be understood Univocally, which allows and leads to the reformed view of Omni-benevolence being Voluntaristic.

C. S. Lewis' view of the Omnipotence of God in relation to the fall, ends in the philosophy of Intellectualism. Classical Theists agree with Aquinas that the attribute of Omnipotence is to be understood analogically, which leads to the Classical Theist's view of intellectualism as it relates to the Omni-benevolence of God. This view on Omnipotence is even called "Thomism" after Aquinas.

There is another curious result from the reformed view that God is sovereign over His Love. In their struggle to find an alternative to Calvinism, some Arminians have used the same reasoning as Calvinists but with different attributes. When sovereignty is in the essence of God as Calvinists contend, sovereignty extends to every other attribute of God, not just to Love. Just as Calvinists have what are called "hyper-Calvinists", Arminians have what are called "Open Theists". This view joins sovereignty with Omniscience just as Calvinists join sovereignty with Love. Just as God is sovereign over His love in Calvinism: choosing to love some and choosing to hate others for no other reason than that He wills it, Open Theists believe that God is sovereign over His Omniscience: choosing to know some things, and choosing to not know other things. In effect, saying that God chooses to not know everything that will happen so that He can derive pleasure from being surprised at what happens (I hope this is a fair portrayal of Open Theism). The only point I am trying to make is that the modification of Classical Theism that is made by Calvinists ends up leaving them defenseless against a view that they believe is heresy.

The best argument I can think of to counter Classical Theism and "Divine Essentialism" would be to say that sovereignty is essential to the nature of God, since God the Father is sovereign over the Son and the Spirit. This line of reasoning introduces a hierarchy into the divine essence and is called the heresy of subordinationism by both Calvinists and Classical theists.

Norman Geisler explains the view of Subordinationism:

(Geisler:) "This heresy was held by Justin Martyr and Origen and condemned at the Council of Constantinople (381). It asserts that the Son is subordinate in *nature* to the Father. Subordinationism is not to be confused with the orthodox belief that the Son (Christ) is *functionally* subordinate to (i.e. subject to) the Father, though *essentially* equal with Him." (ST 2, p. 297 - italics and parentheses in original)

For the purposes of discussion I will be referring to the view of C. S. Lewis as Classical Theism. Classical Theists believe that sovereignty is a characteristic of God that is attributed to Him. Sovereignty is not essential to the nature of God because there was nothing for God to be sovereign over before He created. Providence is the means by which God is sovereign -- Omnipotence, Omniscience, Omnipresence, etc. God is sovereign because of who He is; therefore, sovereignty flows from His nature but is not essential to His nature and does not extend to the attributes that are essential to His nature. Love is in the essence of God, sovereignty is not. Classical Theists do not believe that God is sovereign over His love as Calvinists do.

I have found the following illustration to be very helpful when discussing the relationship between the attributes of God. Imagine there is an empty bowl sitting in the middle of a table. Every time you name an attribute of God, you place a cherry into the bowl. Omnipotence, Omniscience, Perfection, Wisdom, Light, etc. A Calvinist would name off Sovereignty, Transcendence, Immanence, Omnipresence, and Ineffability, consider them to be attributes of God, and place a cherry in the bowl for each. A classical theist would not consider these descriptions of God to be attributes of God. A classical theist would not put a cherry in the bowl for each of these. Instead, while the Omnipotence cherry would go in the bowl, the Sovereignty cherry would be placed on the table next to the bowl. Sovereignty, Transcendence, Immanence, Omnipresence, and Ineffability are characteristics of God that are attributed to Him. God is Sovereign because He is Omnipotent, Omni-benevolent, Omniscient, and Wisdom.

Another helpful illustration is to consider the relationship between your lungs and breathing: When you take a breath, we say that you are breathing. I would not look at you and say that you are "lung-ing". Yet, it is because you have lungs that you breathe. The same can be said of the relationship between Love and Grace. Scripture tells us that "God is Love". The Love of God -- which is represented by the lungs in my illustration -- are what the Grace of God comes from. Because God is Love (Lungs), He is gracious (breathing) towards us. As Romans 5:8 says, "God shows his love for us in that while we were still sinners, Christ died for us." (ESV) I would not say that "God is Grace" anymore than I would say that you are lungs when I see you breathing. Instead, I would say that God is gracious and you are breathing. I would also say that it is because God is Love that Christ graciously died for us, just as I would say that because you have lungs you are able to breathe.

Classical Theists are also proponents of a Natural Law. The objection Calvin has to Intellectualism, or a natural law, is that it prescribes a law for the actions of God: Calvin: "And this He did, that no one might dare to prescribe a law for His actions." (EPG, p. 47)

The very first point of Calvinism, according to Augustine and Calvin, is that God must always retain the right to over-rule any of His creatures' decisions at all times, or God is not Omnipotent and Sovereign. This rule prescribes a law for the actions of God: An Omnipotent God must be able to over-rule His creatures decisions; Therefore, God is free to do anything except give real freedom to any of His creatures. This initial starting point of Reformed Theology prescribes a law for the actions of God, the very thing that Calvin teaches should not be done.

This is another reason Sproul should not have listed Aquinas as Reformed, since Aquinas also argued for a Natural Law. C. S. Lewis notes in *The Abolition of Man*, that those that are outside the natural law have no ground for criticizing either the Natural law or anything else. (Abolition, p. 481) C. S. Lewis spends all of *Book One*, in *Mere Christianity*, explaining how the Natural Law is "the foundation of all clear thinking about ourselves and the universe we live in". (MC, p. 13)

The very first point of Classical Theism is that God is free to give freedom to His creatures. It does not matter which theological system you choose, either way you end up embracing a set of rules, or laws, for the actions of God.

CHAPTER FIVE

In the last several chapters I have been attempting to follow Abraham Joshua Heschels' advice and "present the perspective from which the original understanding was done". Understanding the perspective from which the two views of the freedom of God, the Omnipotence of God, and the Omni-benevolence of God were developed, allow us to understand why there are two radically different views of the Sovereignty of God and the fall of man and angels.

Before I continue on to explain how these foundational beliefs lead to two separate systematic theologies, there are a couple of concepts I would like to examine:

First, there is an explanation of why bad things happen to good people that I like to call "The tapestry argument".
The tapestry argument is a popular way to explain why evil exists, or why good things happen to bad people. It runs something like this:

God is weaving a beautiful tapestry over time. Sometimes He permits, or wills, evil to happen, and when this evil happens, we experience it as a dark spot in the tapestry. When we are up close to the tapestry, all we can see is this dark spot. But when we move back from the tapestry that God is weaving, to a point from which we can gain a perspective of the whole tapestry, the tapestry that is being woven by God is beautiful.

I suppose that most of us have heard the comforting platitude that "everything happens for a reason..." For example, I have heard several testimonies of how God drove a person to their breaking point by bringing about some great personal loss, which turned that person to Christ and redemption.

We can easily imagine that without the evil and adversity in that person's life, they would have never felt their need for help and turned to Christ for salvation.

The favorite example used for the tapestry argument is the work of the cross. God willed the greatest evil of all, the crucifixion of His own Son, so that He could bring the good of salvation out of it.

The point being made is that it is good that evil exists, because God has a purpose for it. It is good that evil exists because God has a purpose for evil. It is good that evil exists, and God wills evil to happen so that He can bring good out of it.

I believe that this illustration originated about 100 years after Calvin with Gottfried Leibniz, a philosopher who wrote the book *Theodicy*. One of the central points in his book is that this is the best possible world that God could have created. Since this is the best possible world that God could have created, and there is evil in this world, it must be good that evil exists in this world. Therefore, the best possible world that God could create has evil in it.

Leibniz describes the tapestry argument in *On the Ultimate Origin of Things*. The evils that God wills to happen are the *confused colors*, or *thoughtless smears*, which when viewed from a distance transform into a work of art:

(Leibniz:) "Let us look at a very beautiful picture, and let us cover it in such a way as to see only a very small part of it, what else will appear in it, however closely we may examine it and however near we may approach to it, except <u>a certain confused mass of colors without choice and without art</u>? And yet <u>when we remove the covering and regard it from the proper point of view</u> we will see that what appeared thrown on the canvas at haphazard has been executed <u>with the greatest art by the author of the work</u>."

And again in *On the Radical Origination of Things*:

(Leibniz:) "If we look at a very beautiful picture but cover up all of it but a tiny spot, what more will appear in it, no matter how closely we study it, indeed, all the more, the more closely we examine it, than a confused mixture of colors without beauty and without art. Yet when the covering is removed and the whole painting is viewed from a position that suits it, we come to understand that <u>what seemed to be a thoughtless smear on the canvas has really been done with the highest artistry by the creator of the work</u>."

The "thoughtless smear" by the artist is any evil that has happened. This could be the crucifixion, the holocaust, or a Tsunami.

While Leibniz may have been the originator of the tapestry illustration, the theological groundwork was laid by Augustine:

(Calvin / Augustine:) "That God, the Lord of all things, who created all things 'very good,' foreknew, that evil would arise out of this good: and He also knew, that it was more <u>to the glory of His omnipotent goodness, to bring good out of evil, than not to permit evil to be at all</u>!" (EPG, p. 25)

The following four points are derived from the Augustine quote:
1. God, by His permissive will, permitted evil to exist.
2. God willed evil to exist so He could bring good out of evil
3. God brings good out of evil to bring glory to Himself.
4. Conclusion: God wills evil to happen, so He can bring good out of it, to bring glory to himself.

For a modern day example, the R. C. Sproul quote from chapter three gives an excellent example of the tapestry argument:

(Sproul:) "When evil comes into the world by God's design and by God's sovereign will, -- evil is truly evil and it is a sin to call evil good, or good evil, -- but when God decrees that evil should occur, it is <u>good</u> that it occurs, that is the whole point that has been spoken here, that even though evil is evil, it is good that evil exists, or it couldn't be here, because God ordains it and God is altogether good and he only ordains that which is good. Evil is evil, but it is good that it is here or he would not ordain it. That is not too difficult."

The following four points come from the previous quote:
1. Evil comes into the world by God's sovereign will.
2. It is a sin to call evil good.
3. When God ordains (or wills it), it is good that evil occurs, it is good that evil exists.
4. God only ordains that which is good.

The conclusion we can derive from these four points is that:
1. It is good that evil exists because God has a purpose for evil.
2. Everything that God wills is good.
3. God wills evil to happen so He can bring good out of it.
4. What God wills is good, and God wills evil to happen; therefore, evil is good.

The conclusion of the tapestry argument is that evil is good. Yet,

Sproul told us that "it is a sin to call evil good", and Calvin tells us that "we well know, that nothing is more contrary to the nature of God, than sin." (EPG, p. 187)

We have already looked at the fall in the previous two chapters and shown that God did not permit, or will, the fall to happen. This view is consistent with Scripture and avoids the error of the various "tapestry arguments" that end with the conclusion that evil is good.

Using the crucifixion as a "tapestry argument" that God willed evil to happen so He could bring good out of it to bring glory to Himself leads to the conclusion that it was evil that Jesus died on the cross for our sins.

Scripture teaches that there is no greater love than laying down your life for a friend (John 15:13). Christ laying down His life for us was not evil. This good -- the good of the atonement-- is what God willed should happen. Just as God willed that Adam and Eve should have the good gift of free-will, God willed that His Son should do the good of laying down His life for us to purchase us with the price of His precious blood.

God did not will the evil of the crucifixion to happen. God willed that His only begotten Son should atone for our sins. The act of the crucifixion by sinners was evil, but God did not 'permit' the evil of the crucifixion to happen. Instead, God willed that His son should atone for our sins. The atonement was more than just good! God willed the great and glorious thing of the atonement to happen.

Satan willed the evil of the crucifixion to happen. When Jesus became sin for us, God had to turn away from Christ, as Habakkuk 1:13 tells us: "His eyes are too pure to look on evil." It was Satan who freely chose to attempt to destroy Jesus.

In *The Lion, The Witch, and the Wardrobe*, the witch gained the rights to Edmund when Edmund betrayed his family. Aslan could not simply bound over to the witch, bite her head off, and free Edmund. Aslan had to freely give Himself to the witch and substitute his life for Edmund. The witch had to do the evil of butchering Aslan.

The idea that God has a permissive will, which allows evil to happen, comes from Voluntarism. When we view God through the 'glasses' of voluntarism, we think of Him using His permissive will to allow evil to happen. When something good happens to us, we attribute the blessing to the ordaining will of God. What Voluntarism does then, is divide God up into a bunch of separate wills. Yet, Augustine and Sproul will agree with Aquinas and Lewis that God is absolutely simple (indivisible) in His essence.

As discussed in the previous chapter, Voluntarism is the view that God is to be conceived of as some form of will. God has a prescriptive will, a desiring will, a decreeing will, an ordaining will, a secret will, a permissive will, etc. This view leads to God being divided up into these many different wills.

It is easier for me to understand the concept of 'God is to be conceived of as some form of will' when I contrast it with the opposing viewpoint that 'God is to be conceived of as His attributes' -- His attributes make up His nature, which is over His will -- or, His will flows from His nature. When we view God as simple in His essence, and understood by the attributes that make up that one essence, we understand that only one will can flow from that essence.

Rather than thinking of God as some kind of will, think of God as being Omnipotent, Omni-benevolent, Wise, Love, etc. In this view, the existence of evil came about against the will of God because a God that cannot is bigger than a God that can. A God that cannot do nonsense is bigger than a God that can do nonsense. A God that cannot lie is bigger than a God that can lie. A God that cannot forgive sins without justice being served is bigger than a God that can forgive sins without an atonement; who simply crucifies His own Son to bring pleasure to Himself. This is one of the dangers of the belief in 'absolute sovereignty'. If God is absolutely sovereign, then He could have simply forgiven Lucifer and mankind of their sins, making the crucifixion unnecessary.

The "Tapestry Argument," that it is good that evil exists because God wills evil to happen so He can bring good out of it to bring glory to Himself, leads to the conclusion that evil is good. Yet, we would all agree that it is a sin to call evil good. Since we all agree that it is a sin to call evil good, we should all agree that it is incorrect to say that God wills evil to happen, by His ordaining will, permissive will, secret will, or any other will we can invent.

The next chapter returns to a contrast of the systematic theologies of Calvin and C. S. Lewis.

CHAPTER SIX

"Whatever the LORD pleases, He does, in heaven and on earth, in the seas and all the deeps." Psalms 135:6 (ESV)

    &

"Have I any pleasure in the death of the wicked, declares the Lord GOD, and not rather that he should turn from his way and live?" Ezekiel 18:23 (ESV)

    &

"First of all, then, I urge that supplications, prayers, intercessions, and thanksgivings be made for all people, for kings and all who are in high positions, that we may lead a peaceful and quiet life, godly and dignified in every way. This is good, and it is pleasing in the sight of God our Savior, who desires all people to be saved and to come to the knowledge of the truth. For there is one God, and there is one mediator between God and men, the man Christ Jesus, who gave himself as a ransom for all, which is the testimony given at the proper time." 1 Timothy 2:1 - 6 (ESV)

Since God can do whatever He pleases, and He desires all to be saved, the obvious conclusion of these verses is universalism; However, both Calvin and C. S. Lewis believe that some men will not be saved. Building on top of their view of the fall, each takes a different approach to a resolution of this conflict in scripture because of the path they took to get to this point.

Calvinism believes that an Omnipotent God is able to save all, which means God has to will that some men go to hell. We cannot fathom how this could be good; however, the only God that exists is an all-good God, so we must not be able to know what good is. Since we do not know what good is, we are totally depraved and lack any ability to seek God. As there is nothing good in man, and we cannot understand how it is good that God damns men to hell that He could save, the election of certain men to salvation must not be based on any thing those men would do. The Voluntaristic view of Omni-benevolence along with Unconditional Election lead to the conclusion that the creation and eternal destination of man is foreordained by God to bring glory to Himself. Once you see the logical progression of the system that is built upon the foundation of Augustine's faith, the next step of limited atonement is so obvious that it leaves no doubt that Calvin believed and taught it.

Foundation of Reformed Theology / Calvinism:
1. God is free to over-rule any of His creatures' decisions.
2.   A. God is Omniscient
       B. God is Omnipotent
       C. God is Perfect
3.   A. God knew the fall would happen.
       B. God could have stopped the fall from happening.
       C. God did not need to create anything.
4. The fall was willed, ordained, and decreed by God > Everything that happens is the will of God.
5. No free-will in man or angel.
6. Correct because God wills it. > Created for the Glory of God.
7. Man does not know what good is.
8. Total Depravity or Total Inability. > Three meanings of Faith.
9. Unconditional Election. > Predetermination independent of Foreknowledge.
10. Limited Atonement. > God able to save all - will save all that Jesus died for.
11. Irresistible Effectual Grace > Grace universal
12. Perseverance of the Saints. > Those that "fall from the faith" were never saved.

R. C. Sproul:) "We first face the question, "Does God have the power to insure the salvation of everyone?" <u>Certainly it is within God's power to change the heart of every impenitent sinner and bring that sinner to Himself.</u> If He lacks such power, then He is not sovereign. If He has that power, why doesn't He use it for everyone?" (CBG, p. 35 - underline is mine)

(Dr. Jonathan Gerstner:) "We pray by the work of the Spirit, readers of *The Potter's Freedom* -- and Dr. Geisler himself -- will come to see the truth of the only true God, <u>who is sovereign over all things, especially the salvation and damnation of men</u>." (PF, p. 380 - underline is mine)

     Calvin teaches that God could give the gift of faith to all and has the power to save all:

(Calvin:) "Where God is *not willing* to bestow the gift, nor to show the mercy, it is a display of His *truth* which declares that none can come to Christ to whom the *will* to come is not given. And though He has the power to *draw* them, He draws them not: but they are left to perish." (EPG, p. 87 - underline is mine)

(Calvin:) "Christ also here declares, by this His doctrine, that those are effectually drawn to Him whose minds and hearts God 'compels'." (EPG, p. 34 - underline is mine)

Calvinists believe that an Omnipotent God could make or compel every sinner to choose Him, but God does not choose to do so. If God desired all to be saved, then Jesus would have died for all, and all would be saved. God cannot desire all to be saved since all will not be saved and that would mean that God is not Omnipotent. Calvin argues against God desiring all to be saved in his reply to Georgius:

(Calvin:) "But Paul teaches us (continues Georgius) that God 'would have all men to be saved.' It follows, therefore, according to his understanding of that passage, either that God is disappointed in His wishes, or that all men without exception must be saved. If he should reply that God wills all men to be saved, on His part, or as far as He is concerned, seeing that salvation is, nevertheless, left to the free will of each individual; I, in return, ask him *why*, if such be the case, God did not command the Gospel to be preached to all men, indiscriminately, from the beginning of the world? *Why* He suffered so many generations of men to wander for so many ages in all the darkness of death? Now it follows, in the apostle's context, that God "would have all men come to the knowledge of the truth." But the sense of the whole passage is perfectly plain, and contains no ambiguity to any reader of candour, and of a sound judgment. We have fully explained the whole passage, in former pages. The apostle had just before exhorted, that solemn and general prayers should be offered up in the Church, "for kings and princes," etc., that no one might have cause to deplore those kings and magistrates, whom God might be pleased to set over them; because, at that time, rulers were the most violent enemies of the faith. Paul, therefore, makes Divine provision for this state of things by the prayers of the Church, and by affirming that the grace of Christ could reach to this

order of men also, even to kings, princes and rulers of every description."
(EPG, pp. 151 - 152 - parentheses in original - italics in original)

Since God does not desire all to be saved, Jesus did not give
Himself as a ransom for all:

(Calvin:) "John does indeed extend the benefits of the atonement of
Christ, which was completed by His death, to all the elect of God,
throughout what climes of the world soever they may be scattered. But
though the case be so, it by no means alters the fact, that the reprobate are
mingled with the elect *in* the world." (EPG, p. 150 - italics in original)

Calvin is saying that Jesus only died for the elect wherever they
are in the world and Jesus did not die for the reprobate which are mingled
in with the elect.

(Calvin:) "Be it observed, however, that when I speak of reconciliation
through Christ being offered *to all*, I do not mean that that message or
embassy, by which Paul says God "reconciles the world unto Himself,"
really comes or reaches, unto all men; but that it is not sealed
indiscriminately on the hearts of *all* those to whom it does come, so as to
be effectual in them. And as to our present opponent's prating about there
being "no acceptance of persons with God," he must first "go and learn"
what the word "person," meaneth, agreeably to our preceding
explanations of it; and then we shall have no more trouble with him, on
that score." (EPG, p. 151 - italics in original)

James White explains that Calvin is saying that:

(White:) "... the prescriptive will of God found in His law, ... commands
all men everywhere to repent, with the gift of repentance given to the
elect in regeneration. It does not follow that if it is God's will to bring
the elect to repentance that the law does not command repentance of
everyone." (PF, p. 149 - 150 - italics in original)

(White:) "We do not here refer to the revealed will of God found in His
law which commands all men everywhere to repent: we speak of His
saving will that all the elect come to repentance, and His ability to
perform that will." (PF, p. 151)

73

The scriptural basis for the belief that God commands repentance of everyone:

"The times of ignorance God overlooked, but now He commands all people everywhere to repent." Acts 17:30 (ESV)

(Calvin:) "For when God exhorts men to repentance, and offers life to them upon their return, *that* exhortation and offer are common to all men. But with respect to His own children, God makes *them* worthy of the inestimable privilege of His taking out of them their "stony hearts," and giving them "hearts of flesh"." (EPG, p. 157)

Calvin is saying that the atonement of Christ is offered to all, but the intention of the atonement was only to save those for whom Christ sacrificed Himself:

"All for whom Christ sacrificed Himself will be saved infallibly." (Five Points, p. 39)

(Five Points:) *Christ* "came into the world to represent and save only those given to Him by the Father. Thus Christ's saving work was limited in that it was designed to save some and not others, but it was not limited in value for it was of infinite worth and would have secured salvation for everyone if this had been God's intention." (Five Points, p. 39 - word in italics added for clarity)

(Calvin:) "Now we will not permit the common solution of this question to avail on the present occasion, which would have it that Christ suffered *sufficiently* for all men, but *effectually* for His elect alone. This great absurdity, by which our monk has procured for himself so much applause amongst his own fraternity, has no weight whatever with me." (EPG, p. 150 - italics in original)

The question being asked is: Who did Jesus die for? Is the atonement limited to the elect, or is it for everyone? Both sides agree that the value of His sacrifice is sufficient to save any number of men. Both sides also agree the atonement is efficient for all of the elect. Calvin calls this statement a great absurdity because it fails to answer the question of who Jesus died for, and he believes the reprobate are excluded from the atonement: That Jesus only died for some (the elect) and not for all.

Calvinists have at least two justifications of the fact that God does not desire all to be saved, and never intended to save everyone. The first is voluntarism, that questioning why God wills some to be saved and wills some to damnation is to reply against God and contends that the justice of God is to be measured by the short rule of human justice. (see EPG, p. 116)   The second is the reason why God created men and angels: To bring glory to Himself:

(Calvin:) "The Lord has as *a reason* for all His works: His *own great glory*. This is His ultimate object, in them all." (EPG, p. 105 - italics in original)

(Calvin:) "The reprobate are set apart, in the purpose of God, for the very end, that in them God might show forth His power." (EPG, p. 50)

(Calvin:) "John does not here give us to understand, that the Jews were prevented from believing by their sinfulness. For though this be quite true in one sense: yet *the cause* of their not believing must be traced to a far higher source. The secret and eternal purpose and counsel of God, must be viewed as the original cause of their blindness and unbelief." (EPG, p. 64 - 65 - italics in original)

(Calvin:) "Wherefore we evince no absurdity when we say, that God, though needing nothing to be added to Himself, yet created the race of men for His own glory. And this ought to be considered, and most deservedly so, the great and essential end of man's creation." (EPG, p. 68)

(Calvin:) "...'the wicked were made for the day of evil,' only because it was God's will to show forth in them His glory." (EPG, p. 69)

(Calvin:) "What then is to become of all those testimonies of the Scripture which make the glory of God to be the highest object and ultimate end of man's salvation? Wherefore, let us hold fast this glorious truth: that the mind of God, in our salvation, was such as not to forget Himself, but to set His own glory in the first and highest place; and that He made the whole world, for the very end, that it might be a stupendous theatre whereon to manifest His own glory." (EPG, p. 69)

John Piper describes the primacy of the will in God (which is voluntarism) and agrees with Calvin on the glory of God:

(Piper:) "To put it more precisely, it is the glory of God and His essential nature mainly to dispense mercy (but also wrath, Exodus 34:7) on whomever He pleases apart from any constraint originating outside His own will. This is the essence of what it means to be God. This is His name." (*The Justification of God*, Piper, John. p. 88 - 89 - parentheses in original, underline is mine)

(Piper:) "The chief end of God is to glorify God and enjoy Himself forever. God has the right and power and wisdom to do whatever makes Him happy." (*Desiring God*, Piper, John. Ch. 1)

(R.C. Sproul:) "He may do with His universe what is pleasing to His holy will." (CBG, p. 24)

(White:) "Predestination is based upon the divine purpose, nothing else. That purpose flows from the Sovereign of the universe who "works all things after the counsel of His will." This is the Christian confession: God is sovereign over *all things*. Nothing is excepted, and most importantly, in this context, it is beyond dispute that *the matter of human salvation is firmly within the realm of the "all things " that God's will determines.*" (PF, p. 181 - italics in original - quote marks in original)

(White:) "God works all things after the counsel of His will, including His predestining of men and women to salvation. The result in (Ephesians 1:12) is the repetition of a vital truth: salvation is all to the praise of His glory. Any teaching that detracts in the slightest from the glory of God is not a biblical teaching." (PF, p. 181 - italics in original, verse in parentheses added for clarity)

Read that paragraph again with one concept changed: Damnation is based upon the divine purpose, nothing else. That purpose flows from the Sovereign of the universe who "works all things after the counsel of His will." This is the Christian confession: God is sovereign over all things. Nothing is excepted, and most importantly, in this context, it is beyond dispute *that the matter of human damnation is firmly within the realm of the "all things " that God's will determines.* God works all things after the counsel of His will, including His predestining of men and women to <u>damnation</u>. The result in (Ephesians 1:12) is the repetition of a vital truth: <u>damnation</u> is all to the praise of His glory. Any teaching that detracts in the slightest from the glory of God is not a biblical teaching. (PF, p. 181 - underlined words are mine)

(Calvin:) "And as Augustine, tracing the beginning or origin of election to the free and gratuitous will of God, places reprobation in His mere will likewise." (EPG, p. 23)

God created men and angels for His glory. It is for His glory that He chooses to save some by grace, and it is for His glory that He chooses to eternally damn some to show His glory and justice. Calvin will explain the means by which God makes man responsible so it is just for God to damn man to hell: Mercy and Grace.

(Calvin:) "I obtain thereby the next conclusion, that the mercy of God is offered equally to those who believe and to those who believe not, so that those who are not divinely taught within are only rendered inexcusable, not saved." (EPG, p. 79)

(Calvin:) "But how it is (saith Augustine) that God bestows this grace, making some, according to their *just desert*, vessels of wrath, and making others, according to *His grace*, vessels of mercy; if we ask *how* this is, no other reply can be given than this, '*Who* hath known the mind of the Lord?'" (EPG, p. 115 - 116 - italics in original)

What kind of grace is this? R.C. Sproul explains: "The term "effectual grace" may help to avoid some confusion. Effectual grace is grace that effects what God desires." (CBG, p. 123)

Irresistible grace is really not the best name for Calvinistic grace. Calvin is arguing against the monk Georgius when he says:

(Calvin:) "By this argument, then, the monk must be driven to <u>the necessity of making faith common to all men</u>. And this, as we have before abundantly proved, <u>is directly contrary to the mind of the apostle Paul</u>. Our monk will follow up his argument by saying, that according to our doctrine the elect alone have "come short of the glory of God." And how does he arrive at this conclusion? Because (says he) the grace of Christ is poured out on all who have sinned. But <u>I so hold the grace of God to be universal</u>, as to make the great difference consist in this: that all are not called 'according to God's purpose.' " (EPG, p. 150 - underline is mine)

(R.C. Sproul:) "The term irresistible grace is misleading. Calvinists all believe that men can and do resist the grace of God. God's grace is resistible in the sense that we can and do resist it. <u>It is irresistible in the sense that it achieves its purpose.</u> <u>It brings about God's desired effect.</u> Thus I prefer the term *effectual grace*." (CBG, p. 120 - 121 - Abridged - italics in original - underline is mine)

The grace of God is universal, achieving its purpose. Grace always has the effect that God desires it to have in the person this "unmerited favor" is bestowed upon. The effect of grace upon the elect is salvation: It is only by the grace of God that any man goes to heaven. The effect of grace upon the reprobate is damnation: It is only by the grace of God that any man goes to hell. The reason God created man is for His glory. The glory of God is some men redeemed, and the glory of God is some men damned to hell.

This "effectual grace" is irresistible, and it is given to men as God chooses: some are irresistibly given saving effectual grace while others are irresistibly given damning effectual grace. Those that it pleases God to choose to save are the only men that Christ died for. Those that are unconditionally chosen are given the gift of faith by grace. Without this gift of faith, man cannot choose God since man is totally depraved. While grace is universal, the gift of faith is not. Those that are given faith by saving effectual grace are elected unconditionally:

(Five Points:) "His eternal choice of particular sinners unto salvation was not based upon any foreseen act or response on the part of those selected, but was based solely on His own good pleasure and sovereign will. Thus election was not determined by, or conditioned upon, anything that men would do, but resulted entirely from God's self-determined purpose." (Five Points, p. 30)

White makes the point that predetermination is done "independent of merely knowing future events, or, even better, independent of *anything*

78

other than His own sovereign and perfect will and purpose." (PF, p. 67 - underline is mine - italics in original) There cannot be anything in man that would make God save any man since this would make Grace obligatory, and "God is not under obligation to save anybody." (CBG, p. 37) Man must be totally depraved, and God must have created man to bring glory to Himself, to eliminate any reason for God to save man outside His good pleasure. Total Inability eliminates any ability on the part of man to choose God without the gift of faith and regeneration preceding belief on the part of man.

It is important to understand the order of events in Calvinistic Soteriology, and how the word faith has at least three different meanings or definitions:

Reformed theology teaches that:

1. (Sproul:) "We do not believe in order to be born again; we are born again in order that we may believe." (CBG, p. 73)

2. Faith is not common to all men:
(Calvin:) "By this argument, then, the monk must be driven to the necessity of making faith common to all men. And this, as we have before abundantly proved, is directly contrary to the mind of the apostle Paul." (EPG, p. 150 - underline is mine)

3. Faith is the gift of God:
(Calvin:) "Augustine then adds, Faith, therefore, from its beginning to its perfection is the gift of God. And that this gift is bestowed on some and not on others, who will deny but he who would fight against the most manifest testimonies of the Scripture? But why faith is not given to all, ought not to concern the believer, who knows that all men by the sin of one, came into most just condemnation." (Calvin, EPG, p. 21 - underline is mine)

4. Regeneration precedes faith:
(Calvin:) "Hence it follows, first, that faith does not proceed from ourselves, but is the fruit of spiritual regeneration." (Calvin's Commentary on John 1:13)

5. Faith causes regeneration:
(Calvin:) "When the Lord breathes faith into us, He regenerates us by some method that is hidden and unknown to us; but after we have

received faith, we perceive, by a lively feeling of conscience, not only the grace of adoption, but also newness of life and the other gifts of the Holy Spirit." (Calvin's Commentary on John 1:13)

Faith causes regeneration, yet regeneration precedes faith. This shows the importance of using a precise meaning when the word "faith" is used to avoid confusion. The first meaning of faith is "the ability to believe". Total Depravity is often called Total Inability -- man has to be given faith -- "the gift of the ability to believe." Calvin: "I also affirm that <u>our ability to believe</u> in Christ is given to us of God." (EPG, p. 149 - underline is mine)

The second meaning of faith in Calvinism is "the act of believing".

(Sproul:) "A cardinal point of Reformed theology is the maxim: "Regeneration precedes faith." Our nature is so corrupt, the power of sin so great, that unless God does a supernatural work in our souls we will never choose Christ. We do not believe in order to be born again; we are born again in order that we may believe." (CBG, pp. 72 - 73)

The gift of Faith "the ability to believe" > Regeneration > Faith "believing"

All men are totally depraved and do not have faith -- the ability to believe. When man is given faith (the ability to believe), man is regenerated and uses the ability to believe to do an act of faith which is believing. This is how faith precedes regeneration, yet regeneration precedes faith. The ability to believe causes regeneration which leads to believing. Here are the three paragraphs from Calvin's commentary on John 1:13 with this explanation inserted in the text in parentheses:

(Calvin:) "Hence it follows, first, that faith (believing) does not proceed from ourselves, but is the fruit of spiritual regeneration; for the Evangelist affirms that no man can believe, unless he be begotten of God; and therefore (the gift of) faith (the ability to believe) is a heavenly gift. It follows, secondly, that (the gift of) faith is not bare or cold knowledge, since no man can believe who has not been renewed by the Spirit of God."

(Calvin:) "It may be thought that the Evangelist reverses the natural order by making regeneration to precede faith (believing), whereas, on the contrary, it is an effect of (the gift of) faith (the ability to believe), and therefore ought to be placed later. I reply, that both statements perfectly agree; because by (the gift of) faith (the ability) we receive the *incorruptible seed*, (1 Peter 1:23) by which we are born again to a new and divine life. And yet faith (believing) itself is a work of the Holy Spirit, who dwells in none but the children of God. So then, in various respects, faith (the gift of the ability to believe) is a part of our regeneration, and an entrance into the kingdom of God, that He may reckon us among His children. The illumination of our minds by the Holy Spirit belongs to our renewal, and thus faith (believing) flows from regeneration as from its source; but since it is by the same (gift of) faith (the ability to believe) that we receive Christ, who sanctifies us by His Spirit, on that account it is said to be the beginning of our adoption." (My Note: See #1 below)

(Calvin:) "Another solution, still more plain and easy, may be offered; for when the Lord breathes (the gift of) faith (the ability to believe) into us, He regenerates us by some method that is hidden and unknown to us; but after we have received faith (the ability to believe), we perceive, by a lively feeling of conscience, not only the grace of adoption, but also newness of life and the other gifts of the Holy Spirit. For since (the gift of) faith (the ability to believe), as we have said, receives Christ, it puts us in possession, so to speak, of all His blessings. Thus so far as respects our sense, it is only after having believed -- that we begin to be the sons of God. (My Note: See # 2) But if the inheritance of eternal life is the fruit of adoption, we see how the Evangelist ascribes the whole of our salvation to the grace of Christ alone; and, indeed, how closely soever men examine themselves, they will find nothing that is worthy of the children of God, except what Christ has bestowed on them." (Commentary on John 1:13 - words in parentheses are my addition, underline is mine)

1. Faith is the beginning of our adoption and adoption precedes regeneration:
(Calvin:) "And whence is this gift of regeneration, but from God's free adoption?" (EPG, p. 100)

2. (Calvin:) "God, therefore, deems those worthy the honour of adoption who believe in His Son, but whom He had before begotten by His Spirit; that is, those whom He had formed for Himself to be His sons, those He at length openly declares to be such. For if (the gift of) faith (the ability to believe) makes us the sons of God, the next step of consideration is, Where does faith (the ability to believe) come from? Who gives that? It is the fruit of the seed of the Spirit, by which God begets again to a newness of life." (EPG, pp. 44 - 45 - words in parentheses are my addition)

While man is adopted and made a son of God when the gift of faith is given that causes regeneration, it is only after we have used that faith to believe that we "sense" that we are now the sons of God. We were made sons of God before we believed. It is after we believe that we realize that we were already made a son of God. We then begin to act like a son of God, and begin to be a son of God.
When Luther and Calvin say "sola fide" -- faith alone-- they are not saying that man is saved by believing in Christ apart from works. This would put believing prior to regeneration and justification. They are saying that man is saved by the gift of faith --the ability to believe-- when this gift is given by the grace of God. Man is justified by the gift of faith alone, and this justification happens when the gift of faith is given, not when man uses this gift to believe. If man uses faith to believe and be justified, then salvation is works based, since believing is an act of faith, and any act on the part of man is a work, and man is saved by faith alone apart from any works. When man is given the gift of faith, man is made alive, born again, saved, justified, adopted, made a son of God, regenerated and made willing to believe. All of this happens prior to "faith," which is any believing done by the elect.

(White:) "The gift of repentance (is) given to the elect in regeneration." (PF, p. 149 - word in parentheses is my addition)

Take a look back at the end of the definition of Total Depravity:

(Five Points:) "Because of the fall, man is unable of himself to savingly believe the gospel. The sinner is dead, blind, and deaf to the things of God; his heart is deceitful and desperately corrupt. His will is not free, it is in bondage to his evil nature, therefore, he will not -- indeed he cannot

82

-- choose good over evil in the spiritual realm. Consequently, it takes much more than the Spirit's assistance to bring a sinner to Christ -- it takes regeneration by which the Spirit makes the sinner alive and gives him a new nature. <u>Faith is not something man contributes to salvation but is itself a part of God's gift to the sinner</u>, <u>not the sinner's gift to God</u>." (The Five Points of Calvinism, p. 16 - underline is mine)

Faith (believing) is not something that man contributes to salvation, man is already saved by the gift of faith (the ability to believe). Salvation is caused by faith (the ability to believe) and precedes faith (believing).

"For by grace you have been saved through faith. And this is not your own doing; it is the gift of God, not a result of works, so that no one may boast." Ephesians 2:8 - 9 (ESV)

(Calvin:) "And here we must advert to a very common error in the interpretation of this passage. Many persons restrict the word *gift* to faith alone. But Paul is only repeating in other words the former sentiment. His meaning is, not that faith is the gift of God, but that salvation is given to us by God, or, that we obtain it by the gift of God." (Commentary on Ephesians 2:8 - italics in original)

(White:) "There is no reason, contextual or grammatical, to accept the fact that two of the three substantival elements (grace and salvation) are a "gift," while the third, faith, is a strictly human contribution. Paul's entire theology, including the fact that he specifically refers to faith as something that is "granted" to us (Philippians 1:29), would indicate that all three elements together constitute a singular gift of God, for surely grace is His to freely give; salvation is His to freely give, and likewise saving faith is the gift of God given to His elect." (PF, p. 296 - parentheses and quotes in original, underline is mine)

White has the best explanation of what Calvin is saying. It is by the gift of grace that God gives man the gift of salvation when he gives man the gift of the ability to believe, which is faith. Man does not have any choice in whether or not God gives him grace, faith, and salvation. Man cannot refuse the gift of faith and the gift of salvation given by the grace of God. Grace, faith, and salvation precede any believing done by man.

(Calvin:) "The next question is, in what way do men receive that salvation which is offered to them by the hand of God? The answer is, *by faith*; and hence he concludes that nothing connected with it is our own. If, on the part of God, it is grace alone, and if we bring nothing but faith, which strips us of all commendation, it follows that salvation does not come from us." (Commentary on Ephesians 2:8 - italics in original)

The way that men receive the salvation that is offered to them is by the gift of faith; hence nothing connected with salvation is our own. It is by grace alone that God gives man the gift of faith, and man brings nothing but the gift of faith God has given him. "Saving faith" is the only kind of faith that God gives. You do not need to believe in order to be saved, you need God to give you the gift of faith, to adopt you, to make you a son of God, to give you new life, to justify you, to make you righteous, to save you, to give you a new heart, and regenerate you. Then you will perceive that you have been saved and you will believe. Calvin: "The Evangelist says that those who *believe* are *already born of God*." (Commentary on John 1:12) Again, Calvin insists that being made a son of God is caused by the gift of faith that is defined as the ability to believe and precedes the faith that is defined as believing.

It is the forgiveness of sins (justification) that brings new life (regeneration). Man does not believe in order to be born again, man is born again in order that man will believe. Are we to believe that when we are born again from above that we are born a second time in sin? Are we to believe that when we are adopted and made a son of God that we have yet to be justified? That we have to wait to have our sins forgiven until after we have been made a son of God?

I understand Calvin to teach that the answer to all of these questions is "no". Which means that justification happens in regeneration and precedes "faith" or any believing done on the part of man. If man were to believe before justification, this would mean that the will of man has something to do with his salvation. Justification must precede faith (believing) or the will of man, even if it is willing in accord with God, would have something to do with the salvation of man, and this is directly contrary what Calvin teaches:

(Calvin:) "For if the salvation of men depends on the mercy of God alone, and if God saves none but those whom He chose by His own secret good pleasure; there can, absolutely, be nothing left for men to do, will, or determine, in the matter of salvation." (EPG, p. 48)

Calvin supports this conclusion:

(Calvin:) "A little afterwards the same Augustine saith, "Those who, by the all-foreseeing appointment of God, are foreknown, predestinated, called, justified, and glorified; are the children of God; not only before they are regenerated, but before they are born of woman; and such can never perish"." (EPG, p. 24 - underline is mine)

This shows how the first four points of Calvinism tie together: Total Depravity, Unconditional Election, Limited Atonement, and Irresistible Grace. If any one of these four are correct, all four must be correct. If any one of these four are wrong, all four must be wrong.

CHAPTER SEVEN

Foundation of Reformed Theology / Calvinism:
1. God is free to over-rule any of His creatures' decisions.
2.   A. God is Omniscient
      B. God is Omnipotent
      C. God is Perfect
3.   A. God knew the fall would happen.
      B. God could have stopped the fall from happening.
      C. God did not need to create anything.
4. The fall was willed, ordained, and decreed by God > Everything that happens is the will of God.
5. No free-will in man or angel.
6. Correct because God wills it. > Created for the Glory of God.
7. Man does not know what good is.
8. Total Depravity or Total Inability. > Three meanings of Faith.
9. Unconditional Election. > Predetermination independent of Foreknowledge.
10. Limited Atonement. > God able to save all - will save all that Jesus died for.
11. Irresistible Effectual Grace > Grace universal
12. Perseverance of the Saints. > Those that "fall from the faith" were never saved.

      The last chapter documented the order of events in salvation held by Calvin. Faith causes regeneration which causes faith. It is the first "faith" that is meant by Augustine, Luther, and Calvin when they say justification is by faith alone:

1. The gift of faith causes:
    A. Adoption
    B. Made a son of God
    C. Given a new heart
    D. Made alive
    E. Given the gift of repentance
    F. Born Again
    G. Salvation

H. Justification
I. Redemption
J. Regeneration

2. Man uses the faith he has just been given to sense that he has been saved, etc. and of course man "believes".
It is safe to agree with Calvinists that the reformed view of salvation is "monergistic". R. C. Sproul explains:

(Sproul:) "When we say that regeneration is monergistic, we mean that only one party is doing the work. That party is God the Holy Spirit. He regenerates us; we cannot do it ourselves or even help Him with the task." (CBG, pp. 117 - 118)

The issue that needs to be addressed is whether or not the reformed view of monergism is "coercive" or "persuasive". Calvinists first argue that man is totally unable to come to Christ, that man must be "compelled," his will "violated." Then they argue that no one is dragged kicking and screaming into heaven. That regeneration is "persuasive" since coercion is "external" and the work of God on man is "internal".
R. C. Sproul explains that God could save all:

(Sproul:) "Certainly it is within God's power to change the heart of every impenitent sinner and bring that sinner to Himself. If He lacks such power, then He is not sovereign. If He has that power, why doesn't He use it for everyone?" (CBG, p. 35)

Sproul continues on the describe God as violating the will of man:

(Sproul:) "The question remains. Why does God only save some? If we grant that God can save men by violating their wills, why then does He not violate everybody's will and bring them all to salvation?" (CBG, p. 36 - underline is mine)

(Sproul:) "The only answer I can give to this question is that I don't know. I have no idea why God saves some but not all. I don't doubt for a moment that God has the power to save all, but I know that He does not choose to save all. I don't know why.

One thing I do know. If it pleases God to save some and not all, there is nothing wrong with that. God is not under obligation to save anybody. If He chooses to save some, that in no way obligates Him to save the rest. Again the Bible insists that it is God's divine prerogative to have mercy upon whom He will have mercy." (CBG, p. 37 - underline is mine)

This is the "mystery" of the Reformed faith: Why a God that can compel every single person into salvation does not chose to do so. This mystery is not just why God chose to love Jacob and hate Esau, it is a mystery why God chose to love Pat and hate Jamie. Substitute whatever names you like.

R. C. Sproul continues on to teach the view that regeneration comes before believing:

(Sproul:) "The Reformed view of predestination teaches that before a person can choose Christ his heart must be changed. He must be born again." (CBG, p. 72)

(Sproul) "One does not first believe, then become reborn, and then be ushered into the kingdom." (CBG, p. 72)

(Sproul:) "A cardinal point of Reformed theology is the maxim; 'Regeneration precedes faith'." (CBG, p. 72)

(Sproul:) "We do not believe in order to be born again; we are born again in order that we may believe." (CBG, p. 73)

"And you were dead in the trespasses and sins in which you once walked." Ephesians 2:1 - 2a (ESV)

"No one can come to me unless the Father who sent me draws him. And I will raise him up on the last day." John 6:44 (ESV)

R. C. Sproul on the meaning of the word "draw" in John 6:44: (Sproul:) "The Greek word used here is *elko*. Kittel's *Theological Dictionary of the New Testament* defines it to mean to compel by irresistible superiority. Linguistically and lexicographically, the word means "to compel"." (CBG, p. 69 - underline is mine - italics in original)

R. C. Sproul discusses total depravity or total inability:

(Sproul:) "Paul says the man is dead. He is not merely drowning, he has already sunk to the bottom of the sea. It is futile to throw a life preserver to a man who has already drowned. If I understand Paul, I hear him saying that God dives into the water and pulls a dead man from the bottom of the sea and then performs a divine act of mouth-to-mouth resuscitation. He breathes into the dead man new life." (CBG, p. 116)

Calvin agrees with Augustine and Sproul that drawing means compelling:

(Calvin:) "Christ also here declares, by this His doctrine, that those are effectually drawn to Him whose minds and hearts God 'compels'." (EPG, p. 34 - quotation marks in original)

Calvin gives a description of monergistic conversion, also describing repentance as the work of God which is accomplished in regeneration:

(Calvin:) "Whether or not repentance is *His* own work, ought not to be brought into controversy. So evidently true is that which Augustine says: "Those whom the Lord wills to be converted, He converts Himself; who not only makes willing ones, out of them who were unwilling, but makes also sheep out of wolves, and martyrs out of persecutors, transforming them by His all-powerful grace"." (EPG, p. 63 - italics in original)

Calvin describes the order of events regarding faith and describes man as being made to believe:

(Calvin:) "Wherefore, if faith (believing) be the fruit of Divine election, it is at once evident that *all* are not enlightened (regenerated) unto faith (believing). Hence, it is also an indubitable fact that those on whom God determined in Himself to bestow faith (the gift of the ability to believe), were chosen of Him from everlasting, for that end. Consequently, the sentiments of Augustine are truth, where he thus writes: 'The elect of God are chosen by Him to be His children, in order that they *might be made* to believe, not because He foresaw that they *would* believe.' " (EPG, p. 145 - italics in original - words in parentheses are mine - underline is mine)

89

The first step in monergism is for God to violate your will and give you the gift of the ability to believe -- faith. The elect have the gift of faith bestowed upon them against their will, they are compelled to be saved. Calvin and White explained the reformed interpretation of Ephesians 2:8 - 9: By the gift of Grace, man is given the gift of Salvation, when man is given the gift of Faith. All three of these gifts are the cause of regeneration and are bestowed upon man prior to man using the gift of faith. This regeneration is what causes man to realize he has been saved and use the faith he was just given to believe. Once man is given the gift of faith, he must use it to believe; Otherwise, the effectual grace of God is resistible.

R. C. Sproul:) "If God has no right of coercion, then He has no right of governing His creation." (CBG, p. 42)

R. C. Sproul:) "Is it possible for a person to receive the grace of regeneration and still not come to faith?.....
The Calvinist answers with an emphatic "No!"
The term *irresistible grace* is misleading. Calvinists all believe that men can and do resist the grace of God. The question is, "Can the grace of regeneration fail to accomplish its purpose?" Remember that spiritually dead people are still biologically alive. They still have a will that is disinclined toward God. They will do everything in their power to resist grace. The history of Israel is the history of a hardhearted and stiff-necked people who resisted God's grace repeatedly.
God's grace is resistible in the sense that we can and do resist it. It is irresistible in the sense that it achieves its purpose. It brings about God's desired effect. Thus I prefer the term *effectual grace*.
We are speaking of the grace of regeneration. We remember that in regeneration God creates in us a desire for Himself. But when we have that desire planted in us, we will continue to function as we always have functioned, making our choices according to the strongest motivation at the moment. If God gives us a desire for Christ we will act according to that desire. We will most certainly choose the object of that desire; we will choose Christ. When God makes us spiritually alive we become spiritually alive. It is not merely the possibility of becoming spiritually alive that God creates. He creates spiritual life within us. When He calls something into being, it comes into being.

We speak of the *inward call* of God. The inward call of God is as powerful and effective as His call to create the world. God did not invite the world into existence. By divine mandate He called out, "Let there be light!" And there was light. It could not have been otherwise. The light *had* to begin to shine.

Could Lazarus have stayed in the tomb when Jesus called him out? Jesus cried, "Lazarus, come forth!" The man broke out of his grave clothes and came out of the tomb. When God creates, He exercises a power that only God has. He alone has the power to bring something out of nothing and life out of death." (CBG, pp. 120 - 121 - italics and quotes in original, Abridged)

Calvin explains that the grace of God is universal:

(Calvin:) "I so hold the grace of God to be universal, as to make the great difference consist in this: that *all* are not called 'according to God's purpose.' " (EPG, p. 150 - italics and quotes in original)

Once man is regenerated against his will, he freely chooses Christ, otherwise; the grace of God and His gift of faith is resistible. The elect are "made willing to believe". This is like a man that is compelled to exit a plane without a parachute five hundred feet above ground. The only choice the man has is to freely choose to fall to the ground. In this analogy, the man is already saved before he is thrown from the plane.

R. C. Sproul agrees with Calvin on man being made willing to believe and begins to argue that this compulsion is persuasive instead of coercive. Also note that redemption precedes any believing done by man:

(Sproul:) "The grace of God operates on the heart in such a way as to make the formerly unwilling sinner willing. The redeemed person chooses Christ because he wants to choose Christ. The person now wills Christ because God has created a new spirit within the person. God makes the will righteous by removing the hardness of the heart and converting an opposing will." (WTB, pp. 65 - 66)

R. C. Sproul:) "Calvinism does not teach and never has taught that God brings people kicking and screaming into the kingdom or has ever excluded anyone who wanted to be there. Remember that the cardinal point of the Reformed doctrine of predestination rests on the biblical teaching of man's spiritual death. Natural man does not want Christ. He will only want Christ if God plants a desire for Christ in his heart. Once that desire is planted, those who come to Christ do not come kicking and screaming against their wills. They come because they want to come. They now desire Jesus. They rush to the Savior. The whole point of irresistible grace is that <u>rebirth quickens someone to spiritual life</u> in such a way that Jesus is now seen in His irresistible sweetness. Jesus is irresistible <u>to those who have been made alive</u> to the things of God. Every soul whose heart <u>beats with the life of God within it</u> longs for the living Christ. All whom the Father gives to Christ come to Christ (John 6:37)." (CBG, pp. 122 - 123 - underline is mine)

I can agree with Sproul that Calvinists do not teach that God brings people kicking and screaming into heaven. This is simply the right answer to a different question. The question being asked is: Does Calvinism teach that God makes man accept the gift of salvation and the gift of faith against the will of man? Does Calvinism teach that God violates the will of man? Does Calvinism teach that God compels man to be regenerated? Does God force man to freely choose him? Calvin and Sproul teach that the answer to every one of these questions is "yes".

R. C. Sproul:) "We have already shown that Jesus explicitly and unambiguously taught that no man has the ability to come to Him without God doing something to give him that ability, namely drawing him." (CBG, p. 74 - remember that draw means "to compel by irresistible superiority")

(Calvin:) "For if the salvation of men depends on the mercy of God alone, and if God saves none but those whom He chose by His own secret good pleasure, there can absolutely be nothing left for men to do, will, or determine, in the matter of salvation." (EPG, p. 48)
If believing precedes justification, then the will of man is involved in the matter of salvation. Teaching that man is "made willing to believe" implies that belief precedes justification, which contradicts man having nothing "to do, will, or determine, in the matter of salvation".
In Calvinism, the elect are "made", "forced", "compelled", or "coerced" into regeneration. After regeneration, the elect perceive that they have been justified, adopted, made a son of God, made righteous, and given the gift of salvation. Then the elect choose to believe in God. Calvinists

92

do not say that the elect choose for God to force them to believe. It is the exact opposite. God forces the gift of faith and salvation upon the elect so the elect will believe in God. The elect are given faith against their will and regenerated against their will. Then the elect will realize they have already been saved and choose to believe in God.

R. C. Sproul:) "We conclude that fallen man is still free to choose what he desires, but because his desires are only wicked he lacks the moral ability to come to Christ. As long as he remains in the flesh, unregenerate, he will never choose Christ. He cannot choose Christ precisely because he cannot act against his own will. He has no desire for Christ. He cannot choose what he does not desire. His fall is great. It is so great that only the effectual grace of God working in his heart can bring him to faith." (CBG, p. 75)

Another Calvinist, B. B. Warfield, also addressed this issue. In this next quote, Warfield is agreeing with an article written by Miss Havergal, and arguing against an article written by Mr. Trumbull. Warfield agrees that everything that has to do with salvation is done by God, that the faith that saves us is from Him. Warfield disagrees with any believing being done by man at the initial point of salvation:

(Warfield:) "Miss Havergal means in the excellent passage to which allusion is made, to tell her readers that we are wholly in God's hands, that it is He and He alone who saves us, and that everything that enters into our salvation -- our very faith by which we are united to our Saviour – is from Him and Him only. Mr. Trumbull cannot mean this; his teaching is very explicit that we do our own believing in our own power, while God and Christ stand helplessly by until we choose to open the door for them to work in and on us; we cannot entrust to Him a trust which we must exercise as the condition precedent of His acting upon us at all." (Perfectionism, pp. 366 - 367)

B. B. Warfield continues on to explain that the faith / believing that man does, happens as each man works out his salvation in the process of sanctification. The initial point of salvation / justification is forced onto man. It is a gift that cannot be refused:

(Warfield:) "Man has no part to do toward salvation: and, if he had, he could not do it -- his very characteristic as a sinner is that he is helpless, that he is "lost." He is very active indeed in the process of his salvation, for this activity is of the substance of his salvation: he works out his own salvation, but only as God works in him the willing and the doing according to His own good pleasure. It is not true that "God forces salvation on no man". It would be truer to say that no man is saved on whom God does not force salvation -- though the language would not be exact. It is not true that the "eternal life in Christ Jesus our Lord" which is the "free gift of God" is merely put at our option and "our wills are free" to accept or reject it. Our wills are free enough, but they are hopelessly biased to its rejection and will certainly reject it so long as it is only an "offer". But it is not true that God's free gift of eternal life to His people is only an "offer": it is a "gift" -- and what God gives He does not merely place at our disposal to be accepted or rejected as we may chance to choose, but "gives", makes ours. As He gave life to Lazarus and wholeness to the man with the withered hand. It was not in the power of Lazarus to reject -- it was not in his power to accept -- the gift of life which Christ gave him; nor is it in the power of dead souls to reject life -- or to "accept" it -- when God "gives" it to them. The God in whom we trust is a God who quickens the dead and commands the things that are not as though they were." (Perfectionism, p. 392 - underline is mine - quotes in original)

After explaining how regeneration is against the will of man and is done by compulsion, Sproul will now argue that this coercion is not coercive but persuasive:

(Sproul:) "To say that we always choose according to our strongest inclination at the moment is to say that we always choose what we want. At every point of choice we are free and self-determined. To be self-determined is not the same thing as *determinism*. Determinism means that we are forced or coerced to things by external forces. External forces can, as we have seen, severely limit our options, but they cannot destroy choice altogether. They cannot impose delight in things we hate. When that happens, when hatred turns to delight, it is a matter of persuasion, not coercion. I cannot be forced to do what I take delight in doing already." (CBG, p. 59 - italics in original)

The third rule of logic is the Law of the excluded middle: it is either A or non-A: It is either God or not God we are speaking about. An act is either forced or free. It cannot be both forced and free at the same time and in the same sense.

Sproul is trying to get around the law of the excluded middle, by saying that there are two actions in this description, not a single act. The first act is God coercing the elect to be regenerated. The second act is free -- the elect choosing God. Calvinists would disagree that God forces anyone to choose Him. Once God "makes" the elect willing, the elect are "willing to believe," and the elect will freely choose God.

The argument is that grace is an internal force, not an external force; However, The grace that makes man willing comes from God, not from man, so this grace must have been external from man, even if it does not begin to work until it is inside man. This kind of reasoning would mean that capital punishment via lethal injection is not coercive, but persuasive, since the chemicals work on the internal organs. To say that the analogy does not hold true since the prisoner does not want to die would mean that Jack Kevorkian was innocent.

I agree that Calvinists do not believe that man is dragged kicking and screaming into heaven. The point is that Calvinists do believe that man is dragged kicking and screaming into salvation, justification, and regeneration when the gift of faith is bestowed on man against the will of man. If the cause (the gift of faith and regeneration) of the inevitable effect (belief) is coercive (with no ability to choose otherwise), then the effect was coerced.

C. S. Lewis succinctly objects to Sprouls argument:

(Lewis:) "Again, the freedom of a creature must mean freedom to choose: and choice implies the existence of things to choose between." (POP, p. 380)

Consider two possible meanings of the following lament of Jesus:

Matthew 23:37 "O Jerusalem, Jerusalem, the city that kills the prophets and stones those who are sent to it! How often would I have gathered your children together as a hen gathers her brood under her wings, and you would not!" (ESV - underline is mine)

If Calvinism is correct, Jesus should have said: How often would I have gathered your children together as a hen gathers her brood under her wings, but I would not make you willing to believe.

I certainly hope that you can understand why I believe Calvinism teaches "coercive monergism" rather than "persuasive monergism". It is very likely that modern day Calvinists do not agree with Calvin on "justification by faith alone". In the explanation of faith > regeneration > faith, the view held during the reformation was that justification happened in the first faith. It appears that modern day Calvinists teach that justification happens after the second faith, or believing. This is why Sproul describes man as choosing Jesus after regeneration which makes salvation persuasive. White also argues for both views:

(White:) "This is the soil from which springs the Reformed emphasis upon *sola fide*, "faith alone," the truth that one is justified not by any meritorious action or work but by faith in Jesus Christ alone. *One cannot claim to be faithful to the Reformation by crying "sola fide" when the foundation of that call is abandoned.* The truth that God saves by Himself, by His *own* power, on the basis of His *own* will, *defines* the message of the Reformers." (PF, p. 36 - italics and quotes in original)

In the first sentence White describes justification by believing in Jesus - which is the second faith in the reformed formula. This would mean that justification does not happen in regeneration since believing precedes justification Then White continues on to agree with Calvin that God does everything, which indicates that justification is caused by the first faith in the formula and happens in regeneration. The first way is coercive monergism since it is done against the will of man without any choice on the part of man. The second way is also coercive monergism since there is no ability to respond one way or the other. I am not sure how much clearer Sproul can be that man lacks the ability to respond one way or the other in regeneration. I am not sure how much clearer Sproul can be that man lacks the ability to respond one way or the other after regeneration: Man must believe.

This brings us to the question of what ability does man have regarding salvation? Is man totally depraved, completely unable to choose God, or does man have an impaired ability to choose God.

R. C. Sproul explains the Calvinist view very succinctly and precisely in a chart on p. 66 of *Chosen By God*: "Post-Fall Man: "able to sin" and "unable to not sin".

This quote shows Calvin agreeing that man can do nothing else but sin:

(Calvin:) "Whereas I maintain that they have heaped evil deeds upon evil deeds throughout their lives, *because*, being essentially depraved by their birth in sin, they could do nothing else *but* sin. Nevertheless, they sinned thus, not from any outward impulse or constraint, but knowingly and willingly from the spontaneous motion of the heart. Nay, that the corruption and depravity of nature are the source and fountain from which all sins of every kind flow can be denied by no one who would not root out the very rudiments of all godliness. But if you ask me the reason why God corrects sin in his own elect, and does not deem the reprobate worthy the same remedy; I reply, the *reason* lies *hidden* in *Himself*." (EPG, p. 101 - underline is mine - italics in original)

(Calvin:) "There can be no real desire of doing good in men, which does not proceed from God's election of them." (EPG, p. 127)

"As it is written: "None is righteous, no, not one; no one understands; no one seeks for God. All have turned aside; together they have become worthless; no one does good, not even one"." Romans 3:10 - 12 (ESV - underline is mine)

Calvinists qualify "no one does good" to mean "no one does any vertical or spiritual good." James White agrees with Norman Geisler that this is an accurate description of the meaning Calvinists take from Romans 3:10 - 12:

(White:) "But they are incapable of any "vertical" or spiritual good and, according to extreme Calvinism, they are totally incapable of initiating, attaining, or ever receiving the gift of salvation without the grace of God." (CBF, p. 57 - Quoted in PF, p. 100)

The ability of man to do vertical or spiritual good is addressed in Romans:

"For the wrath of God is revealed from heaven against all ungodliness and unrighteousness of men, who by their unrighteousness suppress the truth. For what can be known about God is plain to them, because God has shown it to them. For His invisible attributes, namely, His eternal power and divine nature, have been clearly perceived, ever since the creation of the world, in the things that have been made. So they are without excuse. For although they knew God, they did not honor Him as God or give thanks to Him, but they became futile in their thinking, and their foolish hearts were darkened." Romans 1:18 - 21 (ESV - underline is mine)

Calvin explains the reformed view on this passage:

(Calvin:) "It hence clearly appears what the consequence is of having this evidence -- that men cannot allege anything before God's tribunal for the purpose of showing that they are not justly condemned. Yet let this difference be remembered, that the manifestation of God, by which He makes His glory known in His creation, is, with regard to the light itself, sufficiently clear; but that on account of our blindness, it is not found to be sufficient. We are not however so blind, that we can plead our ignorance as an excuse for our perverseness. We conceive that there is a Deity; and then we conclude, that whoever He may be, He ought to be worshipped: but our reason here fails, because it cannot ascertain who or what sort of being God is. Hence the Apostle in Hebrews 11:3, ascribes to faith the light by which man can gain real knowledge from the work of creation, and not without reason; for we are prevented by our blindness, so that we reach not to the end in view; we yet see so far, that we cannot pretend any excuse." (Commentary on Romans 1:20 - underline is mine)

Calvin is saying that we are blind but we see. While scripture says: "For what can be known about God is plain to them, because God has shown it to them." Calvin says that what God has plainly shown to them "is not found to be sufficient":

(Calvin:) "I, in return, ask him why, if such be the case, God did not command the Gospel to be preached to all men, indiscriminately, from the beginning of the world?" (EPG, p. 151)

Yet Paul tells us the opposite in Romans: "For His invisible attributes, namely, His eternal power and divine nature, <u>have been clearly perceived, ever since the creation of the world</u>, in the things that have been made." Paul is saying that what man has clearly perceived in God's creation and handiwork is sufficient for man to reason his way to God, which is why man is found to be without excuse. If the revelation of God in creation is insufficient, then man would have an excuse.

Paul also tells us in Colossians that the gospel has been preached to all men:

"If ye continue in the faith grounded and settled, and be not moved away from <u>the hope of the gospel</u>, which ye have heard, and <u>which was preached to every creature which is under heaven</u>; whereof I Paul am made a minister;" Col 1:23 (KJV)

(Calvin:) "He adds, besides, a confirmation of it, that it is the very same as was preached over the whole world." (Calvin's commentary on Colossians 1:23)

Calvin on the total inability of the reprobate to understand the gospel:

(Calvin:) "What is *free-will*? When the Scripture everywhere declares, that man, being the captive, the servant, and the slave of the devil, is carried away into wickedness of every kind, with his *whole mind* and *inclination*; <u>being utterly incapable of *understanding* the things of God</u>, much less of *doing* them?" (EPG, p. 192 - italics in original - underline is mine)

This is the clearest definition of Total Depravity by Calvin: Man is utterly incapable of understanding the things of God. If the reprobate never do any spiritual good, we must conclude that clearly perceiving God in His creation is evil, and God showing it to them is also evil. If man is able to "see" as Calvin says, or "clearly perceive" as scripture says, then man has the ability to do the spiritual good of perceiving and understanding God, which shows that the belief of total inability is contrary to scripture.

James White contradicts Calvin, and agrees that the reprobate clearly perceive God in His creation and even understand the Gospel.

How the reprobate, who can only sin, and are incapable of doing any good, have the ability to do this good, and actually do this good, is unexplained:

(White:) "Calvinists surely *do* believe that unsaved people *can* and *do* understand the truth of the Gospel, and they universally reject it outside of the divine act of regeneration." (PF, p. 118 - italics in original)

The view of total depravity leads to the belief in restrictivism or exclusivism (See PF, p. 229). As Calvin taught, the gospel is not preached to all men, Jesus died exclusively for the elect, and the gift of faith is only given to the elect. There is no opportunity of salvation for those who do not have the gospel preached to them. Salvation is restricted to those that God chooses to have the gospel preached to, and salvation is restricted to those that He chooses to graciously give the gift of faith to.

(Calvin:) "Every sinner is inexcusable: either on account of his original sin and sinful nature; or else from the additional act of his own will, whether he knew that he was sinning, or knew it not; whether he had a judgment of what is right, or had it not. For ignorance itself, in those who will not understand, is undoubtedly sin; and in those who cannot understand, ignorance is the punishment of sin." (EPG, p. 54)

Exclusivism leads to this interesting statement by Calvin on the eternal destination of some infants to eternal life, and other infants to eternal damnation:

(Calvin:) "But, if original sin and guilt are not, in the estimation of Pighius, sufficient to condemn men eternally; and if the secret judgment of God can have no place with him; what will he make of the case of infant children who are taken out of this life before they could possibly have performed any of the works of charity above alluded to? Now there was the same natural condition of birth and of death, both in those infants who died in Sodom, and in those who died in Jerusalem; and their works, or rather no works, were precisely the same. How is it, then, that Christ will separate, in the last day, the one from the other, placing the one on His right hand and the other on His left? Who does not here adore the glorious judgment of God, who ordained that the one part of these children should be born at Jerusalem, whence, through the knowledge of the truth they might afterwards be translated to a better life, while the others should be born in that wide entrance into hell, Sodom?" (EPG, p. 99 - 100)

CHAPTER EIGHT

Foundation of Classical Theism:
1. God is free to give real freedom to His creatures.
2.   A. God is Omniscient
      B. God is Omnipotent
      C. God is Perfect
3.   A. God knew the fall would happen.
      B. God could not stop the fall from happening.
      C. God did not need to create anything.
4. The fall was not ordained by God > God chose to give man the ability to choose.
5. Man and Angel's are "Free Moral Agents".
6. Correct; Therefore, God wills it. > Man created so God could Love us.
7. The ability for man to know good and evil is impaired.
8. Unrighteous with impaired ability > Faith - ability to believe - common to all.
9. Election is Predetermined according to Foreknowledge
10. Universal, Voluntary, Particular, Penal, Substitutionary Atonement.
11. Universal Resistible Grace > Each person held responsible for the amount of revelation received.
12. Perseverance of the Saints. > Only the elect believe.

     C. S. Lewis explains that God cannot do what is logically contradictory, and it is logically contradictory to say that God could give man freedom and withhold freedom from man at the same time. C. S. Lewis explains that the doctrine of the fall teaches that "man is now a horror to God and to himself and a creature ill-adapted to the universe not because God made him so but because he has made himself so by the abuse of his free will." (POP, p. 397)

     This means that the fall was not ordained by God, instead there is a "free will" in both men and angels. Free will is defined as: free from coercion, both external and internal, but not free from persuasion or influences, both external and internal in the decisions for which man is responsible.

The will of God flows from His Nature and there is a Natural Law or intrinsic right and wrong. Therefore, "God commands certain things because they are right". And "God's will is determined by His wisdom which always perceives, and His goodness which always embraces, the intrinsically good." (POP, p. 409)

In *Perelandra*, C. S. Lewis describes a new world with an Adam, an Eve, a tempter, and a Christ figure. Instead of a garden containing a tree with forbidden fruit, the first pair live on floating mats of vegetation on the sea and must not spend the night on the only island made of soil. Weston plays the part of the tempter. He has been possessed by a demon and argues for the Calvinistic view that it was God's will that man sin so that He could bring good out of the fall. Ransom, the Christ figure argues against this view.

Ransom addresses "the green lady" who represents "Eve". Ransom says:

"This man (Weston) has said that the law against living on the Fixed Island is different from the other Laws, because it is not the same for all worlds and because we cannot see the goodness in it. And so far he says well. But then he says that it is thus different in order that you may disobey it. But there might be another reason."

"I think He (God) made one law of that kind in order that there might be obedience. In all these other matters what you call obeying Him is but doing what seems good in your own eyes also. Is love content with that? You do them, indeed, because they are His will, but not only because they are His will. Where can you taste the joy of obeying unless He bids you do something for which His bidding is the *only* reason?" (Perelandra, p. 101 - parenthetical words are my addition - underline is mine)

The Green Lady responds:

"Oh, how well I see it! We cannot walk out of Maleldil's (God's) will: but He has given us a way to walk out of *our* will. And there could be no such way except a command like this. Out of our own will. It is like passing out through the world's roof into Deep Heaven. All beyond is Love Himself. I knew there was joy in looking upon the Fixed Island and laying down all thought of ever living there, but I did not till now understand." (Perelandra, pp. 101 - 102 - italics in original - parenthetical word is my addition)

The argument is remarkably simple, When God freely makes a promise, such as telling man that he is free to eat from any tree, God is bound by His nature to keep His promise. It was the will of God to give Man free will, and who are you to reply against God? Calvinists argue that God willed that Joseph's brothers sell him into slavery in Egypt so He could bring good out of it. C. S. Lewis disagrees that it was God's will that the brothers do evil; However, he agrees that God brought good out of it:

(Lewis:) "Even the Church would tell him that good came of disobedience in the end. Of course good came of it. Is Maleldil a beast that we can stop His path, or a leaf that we can twist His shape? Whatever you do, He will make good of it. But not the good He had prepared for you if you had obeyed Him. That is lost forever. The first King and first Mother of our world did the forbidden thing; and He brought good of it in the end. But what they did was not good; and what they lost we have not seen. And there were some to whom no good came nor ever will come." (Perelandra, p. 104)

The Abolition of Man explains the Natural Law and intellectualism. This is the view that there is an intrinsic good and evil. This leads to the reason for creation:

(Lewis:) "We were made not primarily that we may love God (though we were made for that too) but that God may love us, that we may become objects in which the Divine love may rest 'well pleased'." (POP, p. 388 - parentheses in original)

James White quotes a sermon from Charles Spurgeon which is consistent with the view of Calvinism that God created man to bring glory to Himself:

(Spurgeon:) "There is no attribute of God more comforting to His children than the doctrine of Divine Sovereignty. ... Men will allow God to be everywhere except upon His throne. ... when God ascends His throne, His creatures then gnash their teeth; and when we proclaim an enthroned God, and His right to do as He wills with His own, to dispose of His creatures as He thinks well, without consulting them in the matter, then it is that we are hissed and execrated, and then it is that men turn a deaf ear to us, for God on His throne is not the God they love." (PF, p. 36 - 37 - underline is mine, Abridged)

I believe C. S. Lewis may have had this sermon in mind when he wrote the following in *The Magicians Nephew* and argued against the view of Calvin that man was created for the glory of God:

(Lewis:) "It was my sister's fault," said the Queen. "She drove me to it. May the curse of all the Powers rest upon her for ever! At any moment I was ready to make peace - yes, and to spare her life too, if only she would yield me the throne. But she would not. Her pride has destroyed the whole world. Even after the war had begun, there was a solemn promise that neither side would use Magic. But when she broke her promise, what could I do? Fool! As if she did not know that I had more magic than she! She even knew that I had the secret of the Deplorable Word. Did she think - she was always a weakling - that I would not use it?"
"What was it?" said Digory.
"That was the secret of secrets," said the Queen Jadis. "It had long been known to the great kings of our race that there was a word which, if spoken with the proper ceremonies, would destroy all living things except the one who spoke it. But the ancient kings were weak and soft-hearted and bound themselves and all who should come after them with great oaths never even to seek after the knowledge of that word. But I learned it in a secret place and paid a terrible price to learn it. I did not use it until she forced me to it. I fought to overcome her by every other means. I poured out the blood of my armies like water --"
"Beast!" muttered Polly.
"The last great battle," said the Queen, "raged for three days here in Charn itself. For three days I looked down upon it from this very spot. I did not use my power till the last of my soldiers had fallen, and the accursed woman, my sister, at the head of her rebels was halfway up those great stairs that lead up from the city to the terrace. Then I waited till we were so close that we could see one another's faces. She flashed her horrible, wicked eyes upon me and said, 'Victory'. 'Yes,' said I, 'Victory, but not yours.' Then I spoke the Deplorable Word. A moment later I was the only living thing beneath the sun."
"But the people?" gasped Digory.
"What people, boy?" asked the Queen.

"All the ordinary people," said Polly, "who'd never done you any harm.
And the women, and the children, and the animals."
"Don't you understand?" said the Queen (still speaking to Digory), "<u>I was
the Queen. They were all *my* people. What else were they there for but
to do my will?</u>"
"It was rather hard luck on them, all the same," said he.
"I had forgotten that you are only a common boy. How should you
understand reasons of State? <u>You must learn child, that what would be
wrong for you, or for any of the common people is not wrong in a great
Queen such as I. The weight of the world is on our shoulders. We must
be freed from all rules.</u> Ours is a high and lonely destiny."
Digory suddenly remembered that Uncle Andrew had used exactly the
same words. But they sounded much grander when Queen Jadis said
them; perhaps because Uncle Andrew was not seven feet tall and
dazzlingly beautiful." (TMN, pp. 41 - 42 - underline is mine - italics in
original)

Calvin taught that the glory of God is some men redeemed and
sent to heaven, and some men damned and sent to hell. This is the
sovereign God being preached by Spurgeon; However, it was Irenaeus
that said, "The glory of God is man fully alive, and the life of man
consists in beholding God" (Against the Heresy of Gnosticism). The
contrast between man being primarily created to bring glory to God, and
man primarily being created so that God could love us could not be more
stark. The opposing views of the Omni-benevolence of God, lead to
opposing views of the primary purpose for the creation of man.
Intellectualism, the belief that something is correct, therefore God wills
it, leads to an opposing view from Calvinism on the ability of man.

Intellectualism leads to the belief that while man is unrighteous in
the sight of God, man still has the ability to know good from evil. This
view is seen in the following two passages from Romans:

"As it is written: "None is righteous, no, not one; no one understands; no
one seeks for God. All have turned aside; together they have become
worthless; no one does good, not even one." Romans 3:10 - 12 (ESV)
"For what can be known about God is plain to them, because God has
shown it to them. For his invisible attributes, namely, his eternal power
and divine nature, have been clearly perceived, ever since the creation of
the world, in the things that have been made. So they are without excuse.

For although they knew God, they did not honor him as God or give thanks to him, but they became futile in their thinking, and their foolish hearts were darkened." Romans 1:19 - 20 (ESV)

Just as Calvinist modify "no one does good" to "no one does spiritual good". Classical Theists also modify "no one does good" to "no one always does good" or "no one is good enough," which is an amplification of "None is righteous". Classical Theists argue that this is consistent with the overall context of the passage, which is righteousness, and harmonizes the two passages. Man does have an impaired ability to know right from wrong, the natural law. Man seeing God in His creation is definitely good, which means man has the ability to do good. This also means that all who clearly perceive God in His creation do spiritual good, which is what Calvinists just told us is impossible.

C. S. Lewis on the doctrine of Total Depravity:

(Lewis:) "I disbelieve that doctrine, partly on the logical ground that if our depravity were total we should not know ourselves to be depraved." (POP, p. 395)

The issue is very simple: why do the reprobate feel guilt or shame if they are totally depraved? The reprobate feel guilty when then disobey the natural law because they know this law which God has written on their hearts and they can reason their way to that which is intrinsically good and intrinsically evil. This argument cannot be swept away by claiming that this is describing "total depravity" as "utter depravity". The doctrine of total depravity teaches that man is incapable of doing anything that is good. Having the ability to know what good is, means that man is capable of doing good, since man just did the good of knowing what good is.

C. S. Lewis gives a description of the difference between a fallen man and a totally depraved man in *Out of the Silent Planet*. Weston is a fallen man, capable of knowing good and evil. Devine is the "thin one" who is totally depraved and incapable of knowing good from evil. Oyarsa is the good angel that rules in the world where this conversation takes place. The Silent Planet is Earth:

(Lewis:) Oyarsa to Weston: "I see now how the lord of the silent world has bent you. There are laws that all *hnau* (rational beings like man) know, of pity and straight dealing and shame and the like, and one of these is the love of kindred. He has taught you to break all of them except this one, which is not one of the greatest laws; this one he has bent till it becomes folly and has set it up, thus bent, to be a little, blind Oyarsa in your brain. And now you can do nothing but obey it, though if we ask you why it is a law you give no other reason for it than for all the other and greater laws which it drives you to disobey. Do you know why he has done this?"

Weston to Oyarsa: "Me think no such person -- me wise, new man, -- no believe all that old talk."

Oyarsa to Weston: "I will tell you. He has left you this one because a bent *hnau* can do more evil than a broken one. He has only bent you; but this Thin One who sits on the ground he has broken, for he has left him nothing but greed. He is now only a talking animal and in my world he could do no more evil than an animal. If he were mine I would unmake his body for the *hnau* in it is already dead. But if you were mine I would try to cure you. Tell me, Thick One, why did you come here?" (Silent, pp. 137 - 138 - italics in original, words in parentheses added for clarity)

Geisler also argues against total inability and total depravity:

(Geisler:) "Sound reason demands that there is no responsibility where there is no ability to respond. It is not rational to hold someone responsible when they could not have responded. And God is not irrational." (CBF, p. 29)

Reason is the foundation of intellectualism: we have the ability to reason our way to what is intrinsically right and intrinsically wrong. Without this ability, fallen man would not feel guilt, and the Divine attribute of justice would prevent a totally depraved man from being held responsible by God. A totally depraved man has no ability to respond and is therefore not responsible since a totally depraved man could do no more evil than an animal. A totally depraved man would not feel guilty for doing something wrong, since he would not know he had done anything wrong.

This view of the depravity of man means that everyone is capable of putting their faith in God. Faith, defined as 'the ability to believe', is common to all men. Faith, defined as 'believing', precedes justification:

"For what does the Scripture say? "Abraham believed God, and it was counted to him as righteousness"." Romans 4:3 (ESV)

"But what does it say? "The word is near you, in your mouth and in your heart" (that is, the word of faith that we proclaim); because, if you confess with your mouth that Jesus is Lord and believe in your heart that God raised him from the dead, you will be saved. For with the heart one believes and is justified, and with the mouth one confesses and is saved." Romans 10:8 - 10 (ESV)

Augustine, Luther, and Calvin taught that the gift of faith, defined as the ability to believe, caused justification. This justification happened in regeneration, which preceded any believing being done on the part of man. Their "justification by faith alone" was really "justification by the gift of the ability to believe (faith) alone". This justification takes place before any believing being done by man.

The "justification by faith alone" taught by C. S. Lewis is "justification by believing (faith) alone". This view is consistent with the order described in the verses quoted above.

Examining the various views regarding the salvation of Hymenaeus and Alexander illustrates the implications of the view that faith is common to all men or that faith is a gift only to the elect:

"This charge I entrust to you, Timothy, my child, in accordance with the prophecies previously made about you, that by them you may wage the good warfare, holding faith and a good conscience. By rejecting this, some have made shipwreck of their faith, among whom are Hymenaeus and Alexander, whom I have handed over to Satan that they may learn not to blaspheme." 1 Timothy 1:18 - 20 (ESV)

Since Calvinists believe that faith is a gift from God and only the elect are given this gift, and this gift includes the gift of salvation, Hymenaeus and Alexander must have been saved. This conclusion does not fit the framework of Calvinism, requiring another meaning of the word faith.

The first definition of faith is: The ability to believe.
The second definition of faith is: Believing.
The third definition of faith is: Sound doctrine.

Calvin explains 1 Timothy 1:18 - 20 this way:

(Calvin:) "I understand the word *faith* to be a general term, denoting sound doctrine. We know that the treasure of sound doctrine is invaluable, and therefore there is nothing that we ought to dread more than to have it taken from us. But Paul here informs us, that there is only one way of keeping it safe; and that is, to secure it by the locks and bars of a good conscience." (Commentary on 1 Timothy 1:19 - italics in original)

Calvin continues on to explain the fate of Hymenaeus and Alexander:

(Calvin:) "As I mentioned in the exposition of another passage, (1 Cor. v. 5) there are some who interpret this to mean that extraordinary chastisement was inflicted on those persons; and they view this as referring to "the powers" mentioned by Paul in the same Epistle. (1 Cor. 12:28). For, as the apostles were endowed with the gift of healing, in order to testify the favor and kindness of God towards the godly, so against wicked and rebellious persons they were armed with power, either to deliver them to the devil to be tormented, or to inflict on them other chastisements. Of this "power," Peter gave a display in Ananias and Sapphira, and Paul in the magician Bar-jesus. But, for my own part, I choose rather to explain it as relating to excommunication; for the opinion that the incestuous Corinthian received any other chastisement than excommunication is not supported by any probable conjecture. And, if by excommunicating him, Paul delivered him to Satan, why should not the same mode of expression have a similar import in this passage? Besides, it explains very well the force of excommunication; for, since in the Church Christ holds the seat of his kingdom, out of the Church there is nothing but the dominion of Satan. Accordingly, he who is cast out of the Church must be placed, for a time, under the tyranny of Satan, until, being reconciled to the Church, he return to Christ. I make one exception, that, on account of the enormity of the offence, he might have pronounced a sentence of perpetual excommunication against them; but on that point I would not venture to make a positive assertion." (Commentary on 1 Timothy 1:20 - Parentheses in original)

This passage from Calvin's commentary shows the difficulty Calvin faced since he believed faith was not common to all men. This means only the elect are given faith and "faith from its beginning to its perfection is the gift of God". This would mean that God gave Hymenaeus and Alexander a defective gift since they made "shipwreck" of their faith. No wonder Calvin struggled with the implications of this scripture and prevaricated on its meaning.

Classical Theists have a simple explanation for this scripture. Not only does everyone have an ability to believe in something, in fact everyone does put their faith or trust in something. Everyone is indeed worshipping something. This explains how Hymenaeus and Alexander could shipwreck their faith and be turned over to Satan by Paul without losing their salvation. Since everyone has faith, and not everyone is saved, they did not lose a salvation they never had.

Believing that faith (the ability to believe) is common to all men is not only contradictory to "total depravity" or "total inability" but it also appears to put the ball entirely in mans court when it comes to determining who is saved and who is damned. The Calvinist answer to salvation being entirely of God was coercive monergism. The Arminian answer is called synergism: That God and man "work together" in salvation. C. S. Lewis consistently propounds persuasive monergism.

C. S. Lewis teaches that God is sovereign. Faith is a gift; just as life, breathing, rain, and thinking are a gift from God:

(Lewis:) "Our life is, at every moment, supplied by Him: our tiny, miraculous power of free will only operates on bodies which His continual energy keeps in existence -- our very power to think is His power communicated to us." (POP, p. 386)

(Lewis:) "All creatures of course live from God in the sense that He made them and at every moment maintains them in existence." (Miracles, p. 303)

(Lewis:) "But God's love, far from being caused by goodness in the object, causes all the goodness which the object has, loving it first into existence and then into real, though derivative, lovability. God is Goodness. He can give good, but cannot need or get it." (POP, p. 389)

It was God's choice to make man and angels "free". God choose to make man responsible, to be bound by the decision that man would make regarding his salvation. This is the "mystery" in Classical Theism: Why Jamie chooses to believe and Sam does not. This view would expect to find scriptures that teach that God desires to save every person:

"This is good, and it is pleasing in the sight of God our Savior, who desires all people to be saved and to come to the knowledge of the truth." 1 Timothy 2:3 - 4 (ESV)

"Have I any pleasure in the death of the wicked, declares the Lord GOD, and not rather that he should turn from his way and live?" Ezekiel 18:23 (ESV)

"The Lord is not slack concerning his promise, as some men count slackness; but is longsuffering to us-ward, not willing that any should perish, but that all should come to repentance." 2 Peter 3:9 (ESV)

C. S. Lewis sums it up this way:

(Lewis:) "If God sometimes speaks as though the Impassible could suffer passion and eternal fullness could be in want, and in want of those beings on whom It bestows all from their bare existence upwards, this can mean only, if it means anything intelligible by us, that God of mere miracle has made Himself able so to hunger and created in Himself that which we can satisfy. If He requires us, the requirement is of His own choosing. If the immutable heart can be grieved by the puppets of its own making, it is Divine Omnipotence, no other, that has so subjected it, freely, and in a humility that passes understanding." (POP, p. 389 - underline is mine)

It is this freedom that allows us to offer ourselves back to him:

(Lewis:) "The good angels lead a life which is Supernatural in another sense as well. That is to say, they have, of their own free will, offered back to God in love the 'natures' He gave them at their creation. But there is a further and higher kind of 'life from God' which can be given only to a creature who voluntarily surrenders himself to it.
As with angels, so with us. The rational part of every man is supernatural in the relative sense -- the same sense in which *both* angels and devils are

supernatural. But if it is, as the theologians say, 'born again', if it surrenders itself back to God in Christ, it will then have a life which is absolutely Supernatural, which is not created at all but begotten, for the creature is then sharing the begotten life of the Second Person of the Deity.

This *absolutely* Supernatural life no creature can be given simply by being created but which every rational creature can have by voluntarily surrendering itself to the life of Christ.

Christian writers use 'spirit' and 'spiritual' to mean the life which arises in such rational beings when they voluntarily surrender to Divine grace and become sons of the Heavenly Father in Christ." (Miracles, pp. 303 - 304 - italics in original, Abridged)

This voluntary surrender is our response to Him. This "surrender" precedes regeneration or being "born again". It is "coerced" in the sense that we must make a decision. It is "free" in the sense that we have the ability to choose what our decision, or response, for better or worse will be:

(Lewis:) "But to know it as a love in which we were primarily the wooers and God the wooed, in which we sought and He was found, in which His conformity to our needs, not ours to His, came first, would be to know it in a form false to the very nature of things. For we are only creatures: our role must always be that of patient to agent, female to male, mirror to light, echo to voice. Our highest activity must be response, not initiative. To experience the love of God in a true, and not an illusory form, is therefore to experience it as our surrender to His demand, our conformity to His desire: to experience it in the opposite way is, as it were, a solecism against the grammar of being. I do not deny, of course, that on a certain level we may rightly speak of the soul's search for God, and of God as receptive of the soul's love: but in the long run the soul's search for God can only be a mode, or appearance of His search for her, since all comes from Him, since the very possibility of our loving is His gift to us, and since our freedom is only a freedom of better or worse response." (POP, p. 389 - underline is mine)

I believe C. S. Lewis is teaching that God is indeed sovereign, yet once again, even Divine Omnipotence cannot do what is logically contradictory: To force men to freely choose Him. God can desire all to

113

be saved, yet not all will be saved since it is impossible for God to do what is logically contradictory: force men to freely love and choose Him.

The law of non-contradiction: A is not non-A: No two contradictory statements can both be true at the same time and in the same sense. And the law of the excluded middle: it is either A or non-A: An act is either forced or free, It cannot be both forced and free at the same time and in the same sense.

"Nevertheless, I tell you the truth: it is to your advantage that I go away, for if I do not go away, the Helper will not come to you. But if I go, I will send him to you. And when he comes, he will convict the world concerning sin and righteousness and judgment: concerning sin, because they do not believe in me; concerning righteousness, because I go to the Father, and you will see me no longer; concerning judgment, because the ruler of this world is judged." John 16:7 - 11 (ESV)

In persuasive monergism every person has faith: An ability to believe as well as a belief in something or someone that person has put their trust in. The Holy Spirit convicts or convinces every person of sin. This conviction is done against the will of man. Man does not have any choice in whether or not the Holy Spirit will convict him. This conviction "forces" man to make a choice and "Necessity may not be the opposite of freedom"." (SBJ, p. 123)

Man is compelled or "dragged kicking and screaming" into conviction of sin by the Holy Spirit. No one has any choice in this matter. We also do not have a choice but to respond to this conviction. It is the direction of the response to this conviction that God has freely chosen to put in the hands of each sinner. This is what C. S. Lewis described as "our freedom is only a freedom of better or worse response". (POP, p. 389) Man can continue to rebel, putting his trust in money, knowledge, science, education, or himself. Or man can surrender, believe, be justified, and receive the gift of salvation being freely offered.

In *The Great Divorce*, C. S. Lewis describes what it would be like if people could travel from Hell to the edge of heaven. He describes what he sees from the perspective of being one of the "ghosts" who have traveled on a bus up to heaven for a visit:

(Lewis:) "I saw coming towards us a Ghost who carried something on his shoulder. Like all the Ghosts, he was unsubstantial, but they differed from one another as smokes differ. Some had been whitish; this one was dark and oily. What sat on his shoulder was a little red lizard, and it was twitching its tail like a whip and whispering things in his ear. As we caught sight of him he turned his head to the reptile with a snarl of impatience. 'Shut up, I tell you!' he said. It wagged its tail and continued to whisper to him. He ceased snarling, and presently began to smile. Then he turned and started to limp westward, away from the mountains.

'Off so soon?' said a voice.

The speaker was more or less human in shape but larger than a man, and so bright that I could hardly look at him. His presence smote on my eyes and on my body too (for there was heat coming from him as well as light) like the morning sun at the beginning of a tyrannous summer day.

'Yes. I'm off,' said the Ghost. 'Thanks for all your hospitality. But it's no good, you see. I told this little chap' (here he indicated the Lizard) 'that he'd have to be quiet if he came -- which he insisted on doing. Of course his stuff won't do here: I realise that. But he won't stop. I shall just have to go home.'

'Would you like me to make him quiet?' said the flaming Spirit -- an angel, as I now understood.

'Of course I would,' said the Ghost.

'Then I will kill him,' said the Angel, taking a step forward.

'Oh -- ah -- look out! You're burning me. Keep away,' said the Ghost, retreating.

'Don't you *want* him killed?'

'You didn't say anything about *killing* him at first. I hardly meant to bother you with anything so drastic as that.'

'It's the only way,' said the Angel, whose burning hands were now very close to the Lizard. 'Shall I kill it?'

'Well, that's a further question. I'm quite open to consider it, but it's a new point, isn't it? I mean, for the moment I was only thinking about silencing it because up here -- well, it's so damned embarrassing.'

'May I kill it?'

'Well, there's time to discuss that later.'

'There is no time. May I kill it?'

'Please, I never meant to be such a nuisance. Please -- really -- don't bother. Look! It's gone to sleep of its own accord. I'm sure it'll be all right now. Thanks ever so much.'

'May I kill it?'

'Honestly, I don't think there's the slightest necessity for that. I'm sure I shall be able to keep it in order now. I think the gradual process would be far better than killing it.'

'The gradual process is of no use at all.'

'Don't you think so? Well, I'll think over what you've said very carefully. I honestly will. In fact I'd let you kill it now, but as a matter of fact I'm not feeling frightfully well today. It would be most silly to do it now. I'd need to be in good health for the operation. Some other day, perhaps.'

'There is no other day. All days are present now.'

'Get back! You're burning me. How can I tell you to kill it? You'd kill *me* if you did.'

'It is not so.'

'Why, you're hurting me now.'

'I never said it wouldn't hurt you. I said it wouldn't kill you.'

'Oh, I know. You think I'm a coward. But it isn't that. Really it isn't. I say! Let me run back by tonight's bus and get an opinion from my own doctor. I'll come again the first moment I can.'

'This moment contains all moments.'

'Why are you torturing me? You are jeering at me. How *can* I let you tear me in pieces? If you wanted to help me, why didn't you kill the damned thing without asking me -- before I knew? It would be all over by now if you had.'

'I cannot kill it against your will. It is impossible. Have I your permission?'

The Angel's hands were almost closed on the Lizard, but not quite. Then the Lizard began chattering to the Ghost so loud that even I could hear what it was saying.

'Be careful,' it said. 'He can do what he says. He can kill me. One fatal word from you and he *will*! Then you'll be without me forever and ever. It's not natural. How could you live? You'd be only a sort of ghost, not a real man as you are now. He doesn't understand. He's only a cold, bloodless abstract thing. It may be natural for him, but it isn't for us. Yes, yes. I know there are no real pleasures now, only dreams. But aren't they better than nothing? And I'll be so good. I admit I've sometimes gone too far in the past, but I promise I won't do it again. I'll give you nothing but really nice dreams -- all sweet and fresh and almost innocent. You might say, quite innocent . . .'

'Have I your permission?' said the Angel to the Ghost.

'I know it will kill me.'

'It won't. But supposing it did?'

'You're right. It would be better to be dead than to live with this creature.'

'Then I may?'

'Damn and blast you! Go on, can't you? Get it over. Do what you like,' bellowed the Ghost: but ended, whimpering, 'God help me. God help me.' Next moment the Ghost gave a scream of agony such as I never heard on Earth. The Burning One closed his <u>crimson</u> grip on the reptile: twisted it, while it bit and writhed, and then flung it, broken-backed, on the turf.

'Ow! That's done for me,' gasped the Ghost, reeling backwards.

For a moment I could make out nothing distinctly. Then I saw, between me and the nearest bush, unmistakably solid but growing every moment solider, the upper arm and the shoulder of a man. Then, brighter still and stronger, the legs and hands. The neck and golden head materialised while I watched, and if my attention had not wavered I should have seen the actual completing of a man -- an immense man, naked, not much smaller than the Angel. What distracted me was the fact that at the same moment something seemed to be happening to the Lizard. At first I thought the operation had failed. So far from dying, the creature was still struggling and even growing bigger as it struggled. And as it grew it changed. Its hinder parts grew rounder. The tail, still flickering, became a tail of hair that flickered between huge and glossy buttocks. Suddenly I started back, rubbing my eyes. What stood before me was the greatest stallion I have ever seen, silvery white but with mane and tail of gold. It was smooth and shining, rippled with swells of flesh and muscle, whinneying and stamping with its hoofs. At each stamp the land shook and the trees dindled.

The new-made man turned and clapped the new horse's neck. It nosed his bright body. Horse and master breathed each into the other's nostrils. The man turned from it, flung himself at the feet of the Burning One, and embraced them. When he rose I thought his face shone with tears, but it may have been only the liquid love and brightness (one cannot distinguish them in that country) which flowed from him. I had not long to think about it. In joyous haste the young man leaped upon the horse's back. Turning in his seat he waved a farewell, then nudged the stallion with his heels. They were off before I knew well what was happening. There was riding if you like! I came out as quickly as I could from among the bushes to follow them with my eyes; but already they were only like a shooting star far off on the green plain, and soon among the foothills of the mountains. Then, still like a star, I saw them winding up, scaling what seemed impossible steeps, and quicker every moment, till near the dim brow of the landscape, so high that I must strain my neck to see them, they vanished, bright themselves, into the rose-brightness of that everlasting morning." (TGD, pp. 350 - 351 - italics in original, underline is mine)

This man was not "cooperating" or "working with" the grace of God (as synergism teaches). He fought against it. It was the initiative of the Angel that imposed a decision on the part of the man. It was the necessity of a response to the angel that brought about his decision, but he had to decide one way or the other. The man was able to decide to forbear or to give his permission. When he finally acquiesced and gave "permission" there was nothing for him to will in the matter. He surrendered. Gave up. He was knocked back and nearly slain. He did not "work with" the hands of the angel, made crimson by the blood of the savior. It was the work of the self sacrificing Christ on the cross that purchased his redemption. It was the grace of God alone that regenerated him and made him into a new creature." (Note that C. S. Lewis argues against Calvinism when he writes: "Why didn't you kill the damned thing without asking me -- before I knew?").

In *The Voyage Of The Dawn Treader*, C. S. Lewis describes a similar story. Eustace is a regular blighter, always playing the part of Eeyore. Eventually, Eustace is turned into a dragon when he puts on a magical bracelet. He tells the story of how he became a boy again to Edmund:

(Lewis:) "Well, anyway, I looked up and saw the very last thing I expected: a huge lion coming slowly toward me. And one queer thing was that there was no moon last night, but there was moonlight where the lion was. So it came nearer and nearer. I was terribly afraid of it. You may think that, being a dragon, I could have knocked any lion out easily enough. But it wasn't that kind of fear. I wasn't afraid of it eating me, I was just afraid of IT - if you can understand. Well, it came close up to me and looked straight into my eyes. And I shut my eyes tight. But that wasn't any good because it told me to follow it."
"You mean it spoke?"
"I don't know. Now that you mention it, I don't think it did. But it told me all the same. And I knew I'd have to do what it told me, so I got up and

followed it. And it led me a long way into the mountains. And there was always this moonlight over and round the lion wherever we went. So at last we came to the top of a mountain I'd never seen before and on the top of this mountain there was a garden -- trees and fruit and everything. In the middle of it there was a well."

"I knew it was a well because you could see the water bubbling up from the bottom of it: but it was a lot bigger than most wells -- like a very big, round bath with marble steps going down into it. The water was as clear as anything and I thought if I could get in there and bathe it would ease the pain in my leg. But the lion told me I must undress first. Mind you, I don't know if he said any words out loud or not."

"I was just going to say that I couldn't undress because I hadn't any clothes on when I suddenly thought that dragons are snaky sort of things and snakes can cast their skins. Oh, of course, thought I, that's what the lion means. So I started scratching myself and my scales began coming off all over the place. And then I scratched a little deeper and, instead of just scales coming off here and there, my whole skin started peeling off beautifully, like it does after an illness, or as if I was a banana. In a minute or two I just stepped out of it. I could see it lying there beside me, looking rather nasty. It was a most lovely feeling. So I started to go down into the well for my bathe."

"But just as I was going to put my feet into the water I looked down and saw that they were all hard and rough and wrinkled and scaly just as they had been before. Oh, that's all right, said I, it only means I had another smaller suit on underneath the first one, and I'll have to get out of it too. So I scratched and tore again and this under-skin peeled off beautifully and out I stepped and left it lying beside the other one and went down to the well for my bathe."

"Well, exactly the same thing happened again. And I thought to myself, oh dear, how ever many skins have I got to take off? For I was longing to bathe my leg. So I scratched away for the third time and got off a third skin, just like the two others, and stepped out of it. But as soon as I looked at myself in the water I knew it had been no good."

"Then the lion said -- but I don't know if it spoke -- 'You will have to let me undress you.' I was afraid of his claws, I can tell you, but I was pretty nearly desperate now. So I just lay flat down on my back to let him do it."

"The very first tear he made was so deep that I thought it had gone right into my heart. And when he began pulling the skin off, it hurt worse than anything I've ever felt. The only thing that made me able to bear it was

119

just the pleasure of feeling the stuff peel off. You know -- if you've ever picked the scab of a sore place. It hurts like billy-oh but it is such fun to see it coming away."

"I know exactly what you mean," said Edmund.

"Well, <u>he peeled the beastly stuff right off</u> -- <u>just as I thought I'd done it myself the other three times</u>, <u>only they hadn't hurt</u> -- and there it was lying on the grass; only ever so much thicker, and darker, and more knobbly-looking than the others had been. And there was I as smooth and soft as a peeled switch and smaller than I had been. Then he caught hold of me -- I didn't like that much for I was very tender underneath now that I'd no skin on -- and threw me into the water. It smarted like anything but only for a moment. After that it became perfectly delicious and as soon as I started swimming and splashing I found that all the pain had gone from my arm. And then I saw why. I'd turned into a boy again. You'd think me simply phony if I told you how I felt about my own arms. I know they've no muscle and are pretty mouldy compared with Caspian's, but I was so glad to see them."

"After a bit the lion took me out and dressed me --"

"Dressed you. With his paws?"

"Well, I don't exactly remember that bit. But he did somehow or other: in new clothes -- the same I've got on now, as a matter of fact. And then suddenly I was back here. Which is what makes me think it must have been a dream."

"No, it wasn't a dream," said Edmund." (VDT, pp. 473 - 475 - underline is mine)

Eustace did not have any choice but to do what Aslan told him to do. Aslan is portrayed as sovereign and Eustace had to obey and follow him to a point of decision. Eustace decides to try and do the work himself, to cooperate with Aslan's instructions. His own attempts to take part in the work of his salvation failed. It was only after he gave up and did the opposite of working for his salvation, by choosing to surrender and let Aslan do all the work that he was saved.

C. S. Lewis explains the process by which he was brought to the point of salvation in *Surprised by Joy*, which is consistent with the previous examples:

(Lewis:) "I felt myself being, there and then, given a free choice. I could open the door or keep it shut; I could unbuckle the armor or keep it on.

Neither choice was presented as a duty; no threat or promise was attached to either, though I knew that to open the door or to take off the corslet meant the incalculable. I say, "I chose," yet it did not really seem possible to do the opposite. On the other hand, I was aware of no motives. You could argue that I was not a free agent, but I am more inclined to think that this came nearer to being a perfectly free act than most that I have ever done. <u>Necessity may not be the opposite of freedom</u>, and perhaps a man is most free when, instead of producing motives, he could only say, "I am what I do."

Even if my own philosophy were true, how could the initiative lie on my side? My own analogy, as I now first perceived, suggested the opposite: if Shakespeare and Hamlet could ever meet, it must be Shakespeare's doing.

<u>Total surrender</u>, <u>the absolute leap in the dark</u>, <u>were demanded</u>.

You must picture me alone in that room in Magdalen, night after night, feeling, whenever my mind lifted even for a second from my work, the steady, unrelenting approach of Him whom I so earnestly desired not to meet. That which I greatly feared had at last come upon me. In the Trinity Term of 1929 I gave in, and admitted that God was God, and knelt and prayed: perhaps, that night, the most dejected and reluctant convert in all England. I did not then see what is now the most shining and obvious thing; the Divine humility which will accept a convert even on such terms. The prodigal Son at least walked home on his own feet. But who can duly adore that Love which will open the high gates to a prodigal who is brought in kicking, struggling, resentful, and darting his eyes in every direction for a chance of escape? The words *compelle intrare*, compel them to come in, have been so abused by wicked men that we shudder at them; but, properly understood, they plumb the depth of the Divine mercy. The hardness of God is kinder than the softness of men, and His compulsion is our liberation." (SBJ, pp. 123 - 125 - underline is mine, Abridged)

If you need a reminder of who teaches that God "compels them to come in", take a look back at the previous chapter.

Classical Theists believe in inclusivism: that God will hold each person responsible for the amount of revelation that each person received. Every person has the ability to reason his way to God and put his faith in God based on the revelation God has clearly shown to each person in His creation. I believe this is the overall thrust of the book "Miracles" by C.

121

S. Lewis. We are able to "reason" our way to God. If we are not able to reason our way to God, then God is unreasonable. Knowing and believing are two different matters, which is why reason is not sufficient by itself, we must couple reason with experience and 'taste and see that the Lord is good! Blessed is the man who takes refuge in Him!' Psalms 34:8 (Miracles, Ch. 11)

C. S. Lewis describes inclusivism using the perspective of the Calormene soldier in *The Last Battle*. Emeth, which is Hebrew for faithful or true, has served Tash his whole life and cursed Aslan, only to meet Aslan at the end of the world:

(Lewis:) "Then I fell at his feet and thought, Surely this is the hour of death, for the Lion (who is worthy of all honour) will know that I have served Tash all my days and not him. Nevertheless, it is better to see the Lion and die than to be Tisroc of the world and live and not to have seen him. But the Glorious One bent down his golden head and touched my forehead with his tongue and said, 'Son, thou art welcome.' But I said, 'Alas, Lord, I am no son of thine but the servant of Tash.' He answered, 'Child, all the service thou hast done to Tash, I account as service done to me.' Then by reason of my great desire for wisdom and understanding, I overcame my fear and questioned the Glorious One and said, 'Lord, is it then true, as the Ape said, that thou and Tash are one?' The Lion growled so that the earth shook (but his wrath was not against me) and said, 'It is false. Not because he and I are one, but because we are opposites -- I take to me the services which thou hast done to him. For I and he are of such different kinds that no service which is vile can be done to me, and none which is not vile can be done to him. Therefore, if any man swear by Tash and keep his oath for the oath's sake, it is by me that he has truly sworn, though he know it not, and it is I who reward him. And if any man do a cruelty in my name, then, though he says the name Aslan, it is Tash whom he serves and by Tash his deed is accepted. Dost thou understand, Child?' I said, 'Lord, thou knowest how much I understand.' But I said also (for the truth constrained me), 'Yet I have been seeking Tash all my days.' 'Beloved,' said the Glorious One, 'unless thy desire had been for me thou wouldst not have sought so long and so truly. For all find what they truly seek'." (TLB, pp. 756 - 757)

CHAPTER NINE

"For those whom he foreknew he also predestined to be conformed to the image of his Son, in order that he might be the firstborn among many brothers." Romans 8:29 (ESV)

        &

"Peter, an apostle of Jesus Christ, To those who are elect exiles of the dispersion in Pontus, Galatia, Cappadocia, Asia, and Bithynia, according to the foreknowledge of God the Father, in the sanctification of the Spirit, for obedience to Jesus Christ and for sprinkling with his blood: May grace and peace be multiplied to you." 1 Peter 1:1 - 2 (ESV)

The view of "election" or "predestination" is derived from which view of total depravity is used. I will begin with the Calvinist view on election. The London Baptist Confession of Faith (1689) explains that predetermination is done independent of foreknowledge:

"God's decree is not based upon His foreknowledge that, under certain conditions, certain happenings will take place, but is independent of all such foreknowledge."

As far as Calvin was concerned, there were only two kinds of election. The first kind of election is done independent of foreknowledge: God determines what will happen, makes His will happen, and knows it will happen. The second kind of election is done dependent on what God foresees will happen:

(Calvin:) "Wherefore, if faith be the fruit of Divine election, it is at once evident that *all* are not enlightened unto faith. Hence, <u>it is also an indubitable fact,</u> <u>that those on whom God determined in Himself to bestow faith,</u> <u>were chosen of Him from everlasting, for that end.</u> Consequently the sentiments of Augustine are truth, where he thus writes: <u>"The elect of God are chosen by Him to be His children,</u> <u>in order that they *might be made* to believe, not because He foresaw that they *would* believe.</u>" (EPG, p. 145 - underline is mine - italics in original)

(Boettner:) "The Reformed Faith has held to the existence of an eternal, divine decree which, antecedently to any difference or desert in men themselves separates the human race into two portions and ordains one to everlasting life and the other to everlasting death." (Lorraine Boettner, *The Reformed Doctrine of Predestination*, pp. 83 - 84)

(Storms:) "Rather, election finds its sole and all-sufficient cause in the sovereign good pleasure and grace of God. Were election to be based upon what God foreknows that each individual will do with the gospel it would be an empty and altogether futile act. For what does God foresee in us, apart from His grace? He sees only corruption, ill will, and a pervasive depravity of heart and soul that serves only to evoke His displeasure and wrath." C. Samuel Storms, *Chosen for Life: An Introductory Guide to the Doctrine of Divine Election*, (Baker Book House, 1987) pp. 29 - 30)

(Five Points:) "God's choice of certain individuals unto salvation before the foundation of the world rested solely in His own sovereign will. His choice of particular sinners was not based on any foreseen response or obedience on their part, such as faith, repentance, etc. On the contrary, God gives faith and repentance to each individual whom He selected. These acts are the result, not the cause of God's choice. Election therefore was not determined by or conditioned upon any virtuous quality or act foreseen in man. Those whom God sovereignly elected He brings through the power of the Spirit to a willing acceptance of Christ. Thus God's choice of the sinner, not the sinner's choice of Christ, is the ultimate cause of salvation." (Five Points, pp. 16 - 17)

The Calvinist view of election is that God's decree determines what He foreknows. God determines everything that will happen, then God foreknows what will happen in the future since He knows what He has determined to take place. The Calvinist view of "total depravity" requires that this election has nothing to do with any goodness in man.

Man is incapable of any spiritual good prior to regeneration, man is "able to do nothing but sin"; Therefore, there can be nothing in man that would cause God to choose any particular man apart from His good pleasure.

It is often pointed out that this belief leads to the logical conclusion that the image of God that man was created with has been "erased". Calvinists call this "utter depravity", and argue that they believe in "total depravity", not "utter depravity". In the previous chapters, I explained how voluntarism leads to the belief that we do not have the ability to know what good is, and the doctrine of total depravity leads to the belief that we are incapable of doing any spiritual good, which includes knowing what good is. This view is not only contradicted by scripture (Genesis 3:22 and Romans 1:20) it is also contradicted by the Natural Law which explains why there is an "ought" which man knows to do. (See book one of *Mere Christianity* and *The Abolition of Man*). Calvin begrudgingly admits to the Natural Law while explaining how the grace of God is universal:

(Calvin:) "That God indeed favours none but the elect alone with the Spirit of regeneration, and that by this they are distinguished from the reprobate; for they are renewed after His image and receive the earnest of the Spirit in hope of the future inheritance, and by the same Spirit the Gospel is sealed in their hearts. But I cannot admit that all this is any reason why He should not grant the reprobate also some taste of His grace, why He should not irradiate their minds with some sparks of His light, why He should not give them some perception of His goodness, and in some sort engrave His word on their hearts." (Commentary on Hebrews Six)

The view of election and predestination that Calvin argues against is that "election is based upon foreknowledge". This is called the "Arminian" view and the following is a description of the Arminian view by a Calvinist:

(Five Points:) (Arminians believe that) "God's choice of certain individuals unto salvation before the foundation of the world was based upon His foreseeing that they would respond to His call. He selected only those whom He knew would of themselves freely believe the gospel. Election therefore was determined by or conditioned upon what man would do. The faith which God foresaw and upon which He based His choice was not given to the sinner by God -- it was not created by the regenerating power of the Holy Spirit -- but resulted solely from man's will. It was left entirely up to man as to who would believe and therefore as to who would be elected unto salvation. God chose those whom He knew would, of their own free will, choose Christ. Thus the sinner's choice of Christ, not God's choice of the sinner, is the ultimate cause of salvation." (Five Points, pp. 16 - 17 - underline is mine, words in parentheses added for clarification)

In this view God's foreknowledge determines what He decrees: God knows what is going to take place in the future and determines to elect particular individuals based upon this knowledge. Failing to see any other option when it comes to the relationship between determination and foreknowledge sets up a false dichotomy, where we are only allowed to choose between two wrong answers. I have lost track of how many times I have heard someone explain that they cannot understand how their view is correct, but the opposite view is definitely wrong, so their view must be right. For example, "I cannot explain how man is responsible in the Calvinistic view, but the Arminian view leaves salvation completely up to man, so the Calvinist view must be correct". Or, "I cannot explain how man choosing whether or not to believe allows God to remain sovereign over all things, but the Calvinistic view means God is not very loving, so the Arminian view must be correct".

It is a logical fallacy of a false dichotomy to believe that there are only two possibilities when it comes to election and predetermination: "The elect of God are chosen by Him to be His children, in order that they might be made to believe, not because He foresaw that they would believe."

There is a third alternative to predetermination being "independent of" or "based on" foreknowledge. Election may be according to foreknowledge. The best illustration of this is the example of Jesus voluntarily going to the cross, yet Jesus is "the Lamb slain from the foundation of the world" (Revelation 13:8 - ESV). The logical progression looks like this:

1. God knows all things.
2. God knew from eternity that Jesus would die on the cross (Acts 2:23, Rev 13:8).
3. Thus, Jesus must die on the cross. If He had not died on the cross, then God would have been wrong in what He foreknew.
4. Jesus freely chose to die on the cross (John 10:17 - 18).
5. Therefore, one and the same event is both predetermined and freely chosen at the same time. (See CBF, p. 43)

This view teaches that determination and foreknowledge "are coordinate acts in the simple and eternal Being of God. Thus, neither determines the other. Rather, God knowingly determined and determinately knew and willed from all eternity everything that would come to pass." (CBF, p. 257) Just as Jesus voluntarily laid down His life and His sacrifice was consistent with "the determinate counsel and foreknowledge of God" (Acts 2:23) from the foundation of the world. It is also logically possible for man to voluntarily surrender his life to God and have this surrender be consistent with election done from the foundation of the world, before any man had done any good or evil:

(Geisler:) "For if God is an eternal and simple Being, then His thoughts must be eternally coordinate and unified. Whatever God fore-chooses cannot be based on what He foreknows. Nor can what He foreknows be based on what He *forechose*. Both must be simultaneous, eternal, and coordinate acts of God. Thus, our moral actions are truly free, and God determined that they would be such. God is totally sovereign in the sense of actually determining what occurs, and yet man is completely free and responsible for what he chooses." (CBF, p. 53 - italics in original, Abridged)

This view is extensively explained by Geisler in *Chosen But Free*, and in his volumes on systematic theology. C. S. Lewis uses a different explanation than Geisler but arrives at the same conclusions. His position is found in *Miracles*, Appendix B, "On 'Special Providences'". I will not try and summarize or give the highlights of this appendix. I believe you should read it for yourself. This chapter is only intended to give an overview of the three views and to show that which view of election you agree with will be determined by the view of the depravity of man you begin with.

I believe that it will be helpful to look at Ephesians 2:8 - 9 from the perspective of each view of election:

"For by grace you have been saved through faith. And this is not your own doing; it is the gift of God, not a result of works, so that no one may boast." Ephesians 2:8 - 9 (ESV)

Calvinism: Coercive Monergism: For by grace you have been given the gift of salvation by the gratuitous gift of the ability to believe (faith). And grace, salvation, and faith are not your own doing; grace, salvation, and faith (the ability to believe since man has the total inability to believe) are the gift of God; grace, salvation, and faith (the ability to believe) are given to man not as a result of works, so that no one may boast.

Arminian: Synergism: For by grace you have been given salvation based upon your faith (believing). And salvation is not your own doing alone; salvation is the gift of God, not a result of works but rather a result of working together with God, so that no one may boast.

C. S. Lewis: Persuasive Monergism: For by grace you have been given salvation permitted and received by faith (faith is believing / trusting), And the gift of salvation (eternal life), given by grace, received through faith is not your own doing, salvation by grace through faith is the gift of God, voluntarily surrendering (believing / faith) is not a work, so that no one may boast.

CHAPTER TEN

"Indeed, under the law almost everything is purified with blood, and without the shedding of blood there is no forgiveness of sins." Hebrews 9:22 (ESV)

Son of Man. Lamb of God. Messiah. Great High Priest. Son of God. Each of these names gives us another insight into the nature of Jesus. We gain an additional truth from each of these names. While each is correct in and of itself, the addition of each name adds up to a more complete understanding of Jesus. This is how I view the theories of the atonement. There is no one theory that completely and fully encompasses all aspects of the atonement. Instead, every valid theory of the atonement adds a new perspective and gives a more complete understanding of the work of Jesus:

(Lewis:) "Now before I became a Christian I was under the impression that the first thing Christians had to believe was one particular theory as to what the point of this dying was. According to that theory God wanted to punish men for having deserted and joined the Great Rebel, but Christ volunteered to be punished instead, and so God let us off. Now I admit that even this theory does not seem to me quite so immoral and so silly as it used to; but that is not the point I want to make. What I came to see later on was that neither this theory nor any other is Christianity. The central Christian belief is that Christ's death has somehow put us right with God and given us a fresh start. Theories as to how it did this are another matter. A good many different theories have been held as to how it works; what all Christians are agreed on is that it does work. I will tell you what I think it is like. All sensible people know that if you are tired and hungry a meal will do you good. But the modern theory of nourishment--all about the vitamins and proteins--is a different thing. People ate their dinners and felt better long before the theory of vitamins was ever heard of: and if the theory of vitamins is some day abandoned they will go on eating their dinners just the same. Theories about Christ's death are not Christianity: they are explanations about how it works. Christians would not all agree as to how important those theories are. My own church--the Church of England--does not lay down any one of them as the right one. the Church of Rome goes a bit further. But I think they will all agree that the thing itself is infinitely more important than any explanations that theologians have produced. I think they would probably admit that no explanation will ever be adequate to reality." (MC, p. 37)

The following is a summary of some of the various views, the main proponent of the view, and what I believe each adds to a more complete understanding of the atonement.

RECAPITULATION THEORY

Irenaeus. "God recapitulated in Himself the ancient formation of man, that He might kill sin, deprive death of its power, and vivify man." (Irenaeus, *Against Heresies*). Jesus was the second Adam, who lived the perfect life -- overcoming all temptations, kept and fulfilled the law, suffered and died for us, to bring us life.

The ancient formation of man was repeated when Jesus was made flesh:

"Therefore <u>He had to be made like his brothers in every respect</u>, so that he might become a merciful and faithful high priest in the service of God, to make propitiation for the sins of the people. For because He Himself has suffered when tempted, He is able to help those who are being tempted." Hebrews 2:17 - 18 (ESV - underline is mine)

The destruction of sin:

"He is the propitiation for our sins, and not for ours only but also for the sins of the whole world." 1 John 2:2 (ESV)

Jesus lived the perfect life and is the perfect sacrifice:

"For we do not have a high priest who is unable to sympathize with our weaknesses, but <u>one who in every respect has been tempted as we are, yet without sin</u>." Hebrews 4:15 (ESV - underline is mine)

"Do not think that I have come to abolish the Law or the Prophets; I have not come to abolish them but to fulfill them. For truly, I say to you, until heaven and earth pass away, not an iota, not a dot, will pass from the Law until all is accomplished." Matthew 5:17 - 18 (ESV)

"For it was indeed fitting that we should have such a high priest, holy, innocent, unstained, separated from sinners, and exalted above the heavens. He has no need, like those high priests, to offer sacrifices daily, first for His own sins and then for those of the people, since He did this once for all when He offered up Himself." Hebrews 7:26 - 27 (ESV)

The vivification of man through Jesus:

"For as in Adam all die, so also in Christ shall all be made alive." 1 Corinthians 15:22 (ESV)

"Jesus said to him, "I am the way, and the truth, and the life. No one comes to the Father except through me"." John 14:6 (ESV)

THE RANSOM THEORY
Origen and Augustine. A ransom had to be paid, a penalty or price was demanded and necessary. This price, the blood of Christ, was paid to both Satan and God. Satan received the payment of being able to butcher the perfect lamb. The perfect sacrifice of Christ satisfied the wrath of God, as well as His attribute of justice.

"For even the Son of Man came not to be served but to serve, and to give His life as a ransom for many." Mark 10:45 (ESV)

"And if you call on him as Father who judges impartially according to each one's deeds, conduct yourselves with fear throughout the time of your exile, knowing that you were ransomed from the futile ways inherited from your forefathers, not with perishable things such as silver or gold, but with the precious blood of Christ, like that of a lamb without blemish or spot." 1 Peter 1:17 - 19 (ESV - underline is mine)

MORAL-EXAMPLE THEORY
Pelagius. The example of obedience and trust in the Father by Christ, as well as the sacrifice of Christ for man should inspire the same obedience, trust, and sacrifice in us.

"For to this you have been called, because Christ also suffered for you, leaving you an example, so that you might follow in His steps." 1 Peter 2:21 (ESV)

131

"Whoever says "I know Him" but does not keep His commandments is a liar, and the truth is not in him, but whoever keeps His word, in him truly the love of God is perfected. By this we may know that we are in Him: whoever says he abides in Him ought to walk in the same way in which He walked." 1 John 2:4 - 6 (ESV)

"You therefore must be perfect, as your heavenly Father is perfect." Matthew 5:48 (ESV)

CHRIST AS VICTOR

Aulen. There is a spiritual war going on between God and Satan. The cross was the victory over death and leads to the final triumph of God over Satan.

"For this perishable body must put on the imperishable, and this mortal body must put on immortality. When the perishable puts on the imperishable, and the mortal puts on immortality, then shall come to pass the saying that is written: "Death is swallowed up in victory." "O death, where is your victory? O death, where is your sting?" The sting of death is sin, and the power of sin is the law. But thanks be to God, who gives us the victory through our Lord Jesus Christ." 1 Corinthians 15:53 - 57 (ESV - underline is mine)

"This was to fulfill what was spoken by the prophet Isaiah: "Behold, my servant whom I have chosen, my beloved with whom my soul is well pleased. I will put my Spirit upon him, and he will proclaim justice to the Gentiles. He will not quarrel or cry aloud, nor will anyone hear his voice in the streets; a bruised reed he will not break, and a smoldering wick he will not quench, until he brings justice to victory; and in his name the Gentiles will hope." Matthew 12 :17 - 20 (ESV - underline is mine)

"Behold my servant, whom I uphold, my chosen, in whom my soul delights; I have put my Spirit upon him; he will bring forth justice to the nations. He will not cry aloud or lift up his voice, or make it heard in the street; a bruised reed he will not break, and a faintly burning wick he will not quench; he will faithfully bring forth justice. He will not grow faint or be discouraged till he has established justice in the earth; and the coastlands wait for his law. Thus says God, the LORD, who created the heavens and stretched them out, who spread out the earth and what comes from it, who gives breath to the people on it and spirit to those who walk in it: "I am the LORD; I have called you in righteousness; I will take you by the hand and keep you; I will give you as a covenant for the people, a light for the nations, to open the eyes that are blind, to bring out the prisoners from the dungeon, from the prison those who sit in darkness. I am the LORD; that is my name; my glory I give to no other, nor my praise to carved idols. Behold, the former things have come to pass, and new things I now declare; before they spring forth I tell you of them." Isaiah 42:1 - 9 (ESV - underline is mine)

"Everyone who believes that Jesus is the Christ has been born of God, and everyone who loves the Father loves whoever has been born of Him. By this we know that we love the children of God, when we love God and obey His commandments. For this is the love of God, that we keep His commandments. And His commandments are not burdensome. For everyone who has been born of God overcomes the world. And this is the victory that has overcome the world - - our faith. Who is it that overcomes the world except the one who believes that Jesus is the Son of God?" 1 John 5:1 - 5 (ESV - underline is mine)

NECESSARY-SATISFACTION THEORY
            Anselm. It was necessary for Christ to pay the penalty for our sins to satisfy the justice and honor of God which requires either satisfaction, or punishment of the offender:

"He is the propitiation for our sins, and not for ours only but also for the sins of the whole world." 1 John 2:2 (ESV)

"For I delivered to you as of first importance what I also received: that Christ died for our sins in accordance with the Scriptures." 1 Corinthians 15:3 (ESV)

"Grace to you and peace from God our Father and the Lord Jesus Christ, who gave Himself for our sins to deliver us from the present evil age, according to the will of our God and Father, to whom be the glory forever and ever. Amen." Galatians 1:3 - 5 (ESV)

"In this is love, not that we have loved God but that he loved us and sent his Son to be the propitiation for our sins." 1 John 4:10 (ESV)

"And being made perfect, He became the source of eternal salvation to all who obey him, being designated by God a high priest after the order of Melchizedek." Hebrews 5:9 - 10 (ESV)

"But when Christ appeared as a high priest of the good things that have come, then through the greater and more perfect tent (not made with hands, that is, not of this creation) He entered once for all into the holy places, not by means of the blood of goats and calves but by means of His own blood, thus securing an eternal redemption. For if the blood of goats and bulls, and the sprinkling of defiled persons with the ashes of a heifer, sanctify for the purification of the flesh, how much more will the blood of Christ, who through the eternal Spirit offered Himself without blemish to God, purify our conscience from dead works to serve the living God." Hebrews 9:11 - 14 (ESV - underline is mine)

"He has appeared once for all at the end of the ages to put away sin by the sacrifice of Himself. And just as it is appointed for man to die once, and after that comes judgment, so Christ, having been offered once to bear the sins of many, will appear a second time, not to deal with sin but to save those who are eagerly waiting for Him." Hebrews 9:26b - 28 (ESV)

"But when Christ had offered for all time a single sacrifice for sins, He sat down at the right hand of God, waiting from that time until His enemies should be made a footstool for His feet. For by a single offering He has perfected for all time those who are being sanctified." Hebrews 10:12 - 14 (ESV)

"For the wages of sin is death, but the free gift of God is eternal life in Christ Jesus our Lord." Romans 6:23 (ESV)

"Truly, truly, I say to you, whoever hears my word and believes Him who sent me has eternal life. He does not come into judgment, but has passed from death to life." John 5:24 (ESV)

Jesus is the source of eternal life which He purchased by His own blood. It is the gift of eternal life that He freely gives to all who believe in Him.

(Geisler:) "The salvation of everyone was not immediately *applied*; it was simply *purchased*. All persons were *made savable*, but not all persons were *automatically saved*. The gift was made possible by the Saviour, but it must be received by the sinner. In short, the salvation of all sinners from God's eternal wrath is possible, but only those who accept Christ's payment for their sins will actually be saved from it." (ST 2, p. 405 - italics in original)

When I go to the store and purchase a new coat, I pay for the coat with cash; However, I earned the cash by trading some of my time, talents, and health to earn the cash. While it is common to say "I paid cash for it", what is really meant is that "I used part of my life to get the cash to buy the coat." This is similar to the atonement. Jesus gave his time, talents, and life to satisfy the wrath of God and force Satan to relinquish the rightful claim of ownership he has on our lives because of our sin. It is with His own blood that Jesus purchases eternal life and the ability to be redeemed (to be bought back). It is the gift of eternal life that He offers to everyone. This gift is received by faith (believing).

"You are not your own, for you were bought with a price. So glorify God in your body." 1 Corinthians 6:19b - 20 (ESV)

"But false prophets also arose among the people, just as there will be false teachers among you, who will secretly bring in destructive heresies, even denying the Master who bought them, bringing upon themselves swift destruction." 2 Peter 2:1 (ESV)

Just as I could say that I bought my new coat with my time, talents, and health; skipping over the step of using the cash I received from my work to purchase the coat: I can also say that I have been bought with the blood of Jesus, skipping over the step of eternal life.
The Atonement was universal. The scriptures say that "all", "everyone", and "the sins of the whole world" were paid for by the sacrifice of Jesus. Apostasy is denying the one who bought you. This means that everyone has been bought with the price of the blood of Jesus, and everyone that rejects Him is Apostate. You do not have to be a believer to "apostatize" and deny The One who bought you; Instead, you are an unbeliever and apostate: denying The One who bought you.

This is how I understand the Necessary Satisfaction view of the atonement: Jesus atoned for everyone in particular, and for the sins of everyone, satisfying the wrath of God. He purchased the gift of eternal life (Rom 6:23). This is the gift that is offered to all and given upon belief (faith).

The following are the individual components of the Atonement which are supported by the various views discussed above:

UNIVERSAL & PARTICULAR -- Jesus died for every person:

"He is the propitiation for our sins, and not for ours only but also for the sins of the whole world." 1 John 2:2 (ESV)

"But we see him who for a little while was made lower than the angels, namely Jesus, crowned with glory and honor because of the suffering of death, so that by the grace of God He might taste death for everyone." Hebrews 2:9 (ESV)

"For there is one God, and there is one mediator between God and men, the man Christ Jesus, who gave Himself as a ransom for all, which is the testimony given at the proper time." 1 Timothy 2:5 - 6 (ESV)

(Lewis:) "It is an old and pious saying that Christ died not only for Man but for each man, just as much as if each had been the only man there was." (LTM, p. 55)

VOLUNTARY -- Jesus chose to die for everyone:

"For this reason the Father loves me, because I lay down my life that I may take it up again. No one takes it from me, but I lay it down of my own accord. I have authority to lay it down, and I have authority to take it up again. This charge I have received from my Father." John 10:17 - 18 (ESV)

NECESSARY -- Without the atonement, fallen man could not be redeemed and saved:

"Indeed, under the law almost everything is purified with blood, and without the shedding of blood there is no forgiveness of sins. Thus it was necessary for the copies of the heavenly things to be purified with these rites, but the heavenly things themselves with better sacrifices than these. For Christ has entered, not into holy places made with hands, which are copies of the true things, but into heaven itself, now to appear in the presence of God on our behalf." Hebrews 9:22 - 24 (ESV)

PENAL -- The punishment for our sins was satisfied in the suffering of our Saviour. Jesus paid the price for us:

"But he was wounded for our transgressions; he was crushed for our iniquities; upon him was the chastisement that brought us peace, and with his stripes we are healed. All we like sheep have gone astray; we have turned--every one--to his own way; and the LORD has laid on him the iniquity of us all." Isaiah 53:5 - 6 (ESV)

PERFECT -- Jesus was the perfect man and made the perfect sacrifice:

"And being made perfect, He became the source of eternal salvation to all who obey him, being designated by God a high priest after the order of Melchizedek." Hebrews 5:9 - 10 (ESV)

"But with the precious blood of Christ, like that of a lamb without blemish or spot." 1 Peter 1:19 (ESV)

"For we do not have a high priest who is unable to sympathize with our weaknesses, but one who in every respect has been tempted as we are, yet without sin." Hebrews 4:15 (ESV)

"How much more will the blood of Christ, who through the eternal Spirit offered Himself without blemish to God, purify our conscience from dead works to serve the living God." Hebrews 9:14 (ESV)

SUBSTITUTIONARY -- Christ died for our sins and for us!:

"For while we were still weak, at the right time Christ died for the ungodly. For one will scarcely die for a righteous person--though perhaps for a good person one would dare even to die-- but God shows his love for us in that while we were still sinners, Christ died for us." Romans 5:6 - 8 (ESV)

"He Himself bore our sins in His body on the tree, that we might die to sin and live to righteousness. By His wounds you have been healed." 1 Peter 2:24 (ESV)

"For Christ also suffered once for sins, the righteous for the unrighteous, that He might bring us to God, being put to death in the flesh but made alive in the spirit." 1 Peter 3:18 (ESV)

While scripture does not literally say that Jesus "died in our place", the story of Abraham and Isaac allows for the perspective and insight that Jesus, the Lamb of God, died in our place:

"Abraham said, "God will provide for himself the lamb for a burnt offering, my son." So they went both of them together. When they came to the place of which God had told him, Abraham built the altar there and laid the wood in order and bound Isaac his son and laid him on the altar, on top of the wood. Then Abraham reached out his hand and took the knife to slaughter his son. But the angel of the LORD called to him from heaven and said, "Abraham, Abraham!" And he said, "Here am I." He said, "Do not lay your hand on the boy or do anything to him, for now I know that you fear God, seeing you have not withheld your son, your only son, from me." And Abraham lifted up his eyes and looked, and behold, behind him was a ram, caught in a thicket by his horns. And Abraham went and took the ram and offered it up as a burnt offering instead of his son. So Abraham called the name of that place, "The LORD will provide"; as it is said to this day, "On the mount of the LORD it shall be provided." Genesis 22:8 - 14 (ESV)

Additionally, in *The Lion, The Witch, and The Wardrobe*, C. S. Lewis has Aslan die in the place of Edmund. This is certainly a beautiful picture of the suffering and sacrifice of Christ in our place and on our behalf because He loves us; However, Aslan did not die in the place of Peter, Lucy, or Susan. We can stretch the meaning of the substitutionary aspect of the atonement beyond its intent by saying that Jesus died in the place of every person. Yet, he certainly did die to defeat the witch, purchase salvation, and save Peter, Lucy, and Susan. The substitutionary atonement gives us an incredible insight into the worth that God places on each one of us: That Jesus would have died to save any one of us, and in fact He would have died just to save one of us. It is not the number saved that compelled Him to sacrifice Himself, but His love for us.

"Anyone who does not love does not know God, because God is love. In this the love of God was made manifest among us, that God sent his only Son into the world, so that we might live through Him. In this is love, not that we have loved God but that He loved us and sent His Son to be the propitiation for our sins. Beloved, if God so loved us, we also ought to love one another." 1 John 4:8 - 11 (ESV)

(Lewis:) "We were made not primarily that we may love God (though we were made for that too) but that God may love us, that we may become objects in which the Divine love may rest 'well pleased'." (POP, p. 388)

The atonement is Universal, Particular, Voluntary, Necessary, Penal, Perfect, Substitutionary, and Good News! C. S. Lewis brings many of the various elements and views of the atonement together in the following:

(Lewis:) "But supposing God became a man--suppose our human nature which can suffer and die was amalgamated with God's nature in one person--then that person could help us. He could surrender His will, and suffer and die, because He was man; and He could do it perfectly because He was God. You and I can go through this process only if God does it in us; but God can do it only if He becomes man. Our attempts at this dying will succeed only if we men share in God's dying, just as our thinking can succeed only because it is a drop out of the ocean of His intelligence: but we cannot share God's dying unless God dies; and He cannot die except by being a man. That is the sense in which He pays our debt, and suffers for us what He Himself need not suffer at all." (MC, p. 39)

(Lewis:) "The perfect submission, the perfect suffering, the perfect death were not only easier to Jesus because He was God, but were possible only because He was God." (MC, p. 39)

CHAPTER ELEVEN

"I suppose there are two views about everything"
"Eh? Two views? There are a dozen views about everything until you know the answer. Then there's never more than one."
C. S. Lewis, *That Hideous Strength*, p. 70)

Foundation of Reformed Theology / Calvinism:
1. God is free to over-rule any of His creatures' decisions.
2.   A. God is Omniscient
     B. God is Omnipotent
     C. God is Perfect
3.   A. God knew the fall would happen.
     B.
C. God did not need to create anything.

---

3.   B. God could have stopped the fall from happening.
4. The fall was willed, ordained, and decreed by God > Everything that happens is the will of God.
5. No free-will in man or angel.
6. Correct because God wills it. > Created for the Glory of God.
7. Man does not know what good is.
8. Total Depravity or Total Inability. > Three meanings of Faith.
9. Unconditional Election. > Predetermination independent of Foreknowledge.
10. Limited Atonement. > God able to save all - will save all that Jesus died for.
11. Irresistible Effectual Grace > Grace universal

---

12. Perseverance of the Saints. > Those that "fall from the faith" were never saved.

     Each belief in the system of Calvinism or Reformed Theology is like a brick in a stack. Each brick, or belief, is laid upon the brick that comes before it. Each brick inexorably leads to the selection of the next brick. If the belief held in any one of the bricks that are in-between the solid lines is incorrect, not only does that brick fall, but the belief that led to that brick, and the brick that is about to be built upon that belief also falls. This is why it is called "Systematic Theology," everything is interconnected.

Unfortunately, the failure by Augustine, Luther, Calvin, and Sproul to see that their view of the attribute of the Omnipotence of God was based on a logical contradiction has led them to believe in a system of error that is known today as Calvinism.

(Lewis:) "If you have taken a wrong turning, then to go forward does not get you any nearer. If you are on the wrong road, progress means doing an about-turn and walking back to the right road; and in that case the man who turns back soonest is the most progressive man." (MC, p. 23)

Turning back to reconsider the attribute of the Omnipotence of God corrects the error made by Calvinists and leads to an entirely different system of belief. While you may not agree that Classical Theists have the correct view of Omnipotence and therefore the correct systematic theology, at least you will know why the views and interpretations of Calvinists differ from the rest of Christianity.
This brings us to a consideration of the pinnacle of both systems of belief: The perseverance of the saints. Eternal security does not topple with the rest of Reformed Theology since it is supported by two areas that both systems agree on: Election and Omniscience. The logical conclusion of both election being predetermined independent of foreknowledge, as well as election being predetermined according to foreknowledge is that God knows for sure who will have faith and put their trust in Him.

Both systems believe that "justification is by faith alone". Calvinism teaches that justification happens when God forces the gift of faith on man. It is this gift of faith that causes justification and regeneration: the forgiveness of sins that brings new life. Justification (the forgiveness of sins) brings regeneration (being born again to a new life) which precedes faith (believing).

C. S. Lewis also teaches that "justification is by faith alone". Faith (believing), is surrendering yourself back to God -- this surrender requires you to stop trying to do it yourself and let God do the work. It is this faith that allows justification which brings regeneration via the gift of salvation or eternal life. The credit for the gift goes to the giver of the gift, not the recipient of the gift. (How many children have you seen walking around after Christmas patting themselves on the back for the great gift they got themselves by being brilliant enough to believe the package under the tree with their name on it was really for them?)

In *Surprised by Joy*, C. S. Lewis gives an account of his conversion. His account is different from the account of Augustines conversion. The process by which God pursues man varies to such an extent that "testimony time" is a popular way for a group of believers to bond together. Both G. K. Chesterton and C. S. Lewis liken this process to fishing:

(Chesterton:) " 'Did you catch this man?' asked the colonel, frowning. Father Brown looked him full in his frowning face. 'Yes,' he said, 'I caught him, with an unseen hook and an invisible line which is long enough to let him wander to the ends of the world, and still to bring him back with a twitch upon the thread'." (Father Brown, p. 60)

(Lewis:) "And so the great Angler played His fish and I never dreamed that the hook was in my tongue." (SBJ, p. 116)

This is the process by which God draws us to Himself:

"Nevertheless, I tell you the truth: it is to your advantage that I go away, for if I do not go away, the Helper will not come to you. But if I go, I will send him to you. And when he comes, he will convict the world concerning sin and righteousness and judgment: concerning sin, because they do not believe in me; concerning righteousness, because I go to the Father, and you will see me no longer; concerning judgment, because the ruler of this world is judged." John 16:7 - 11 (ESV)

The Holy Spirit convicts or convinces everyone of their sin. We do not have a choice when it comes to whether or not we will be convicted by the Holy Spirit. We are compelled to make a decision. This is what C. S. Lewis means when he writes, "Necessity may not be the opposite of freedom". (SBJ, p. 123). When the Holy Spirit compels us to be convinced of sin and righteousness, we do not have any choice whether or not we have to make a choice; However, we do have the ability to choose one way or the other: we can choose to be convicted to righteousness, or to be convicted to judgment:

"Because, if you confess with your mouth that Jesus is Lord and believe in your heart that God raised him from the dead, you will be saved. For with the heart one believes and is justified, and with the mouth one confesses and is saved." Romans 10:9 - 10 (ESV)

The moment we surrender to God, putting our faith and trust in Jesus, we are justified and given the gift of eternal life or salvation. As we just read in Romans 10:10, believing precedes justification. Justification means that God does not count our sins against us:

"That is, in Christ, God was reconciling the world to Himself, not counting their trespasses against them, and entrusting to us the message of reconciliation. Therefore, we are ambassadors for Christ, God making his appeal through us. We implore you on behalf of Christ, be reconciled to God." 2 Corinthians 5:19 - 20 (ESV)

At the point of believing, we are justified and "put on" the righteousness of Jesus like a robe -- Just as Aslan dressed Eustace. While our sins are forgiven at this point, we are still imperfect and will continue to sin. From the moment of justification on, we will always be viewed through the perfect finished atonement of Jesus. When God looks at us, He sees the righteousness of the Saviour. We cannot be justified or declared righteous a second time since this would require a second crucifixion of the Saviour:

"For it is impossible, in the case of those who have once been enlightened, who have tasted the heavenly gift, and have shared in the Holy Spirit, and have tasted the goodness of the word of God and the powers of the age to come, and then have fallen away, to restore them again to repentance, since they are crucifying once again the Son of God to their own harm and holding him up to contempt." Hebrews 6:4 - 6 (ESV)

From the point of justification on begins the process of sanctification:

"Therefore, my beloved, as you have always obeyed, so now, not only as in my presence but much more in my absence, work out your own salvation with fear and trembling, for it is God who works in you, both to will and to work for His good pleasure." Philippians 2:12 - 13 (ESV)

"But when Christ had offered for all time a single sacrifice for sins, He sat down at the right hand of God, waiting from that time until His enemies should be made a footstool for His feet. For by a single offering he has perfected for all time those who are being sanctified." Hebrews 10:12 - 14 (ESV)

"But now that you have been set free from sin and have become slaves of God, the fruit you get leads to sanctification and its end, eternal life." Romans 6:22 (ESV)

Sanctification is the lifelong process of doing the good works that God has prepared for us to do (see Ephesians 2:10). The amount of joy we experience in this life can be measured in direct proportion to our obedience to God and doing His will for us. The commandments to live a righteous life apart from the pollution of the world are not burdens. Rather, following Jesus will heap up eternal blessings for ourselves as well as being beneficial to us in our life.

Jesus was crucified from the foundation of the world as well as a point in time. God chose the elect from the foundation of the world, yet the elect are adopted as sons at a point in time. The elect are sealed by the Holy Spirit at the time of justification, yet this sealing is for a future time when we take possession of the inheritance we have been promised. The elect are also considered justified (declared righteous) at a point in time, yet we will experience justification (being made righteous) at a future point in time when we are judged and glorified.

"In Him you also, when you heard the word of truth, the gospel of your salvation, and believed in Him, were sealed with the promised Holy Spirit, who is the guarantee of our inheritance until we acquire possession of it, to the praise of his glory." Ephesians 1:13 - 14 (ESV)

"When the Son of Man comes in his glory, and all the angels with Him, then He will sit on His glorious throne. Before Him will be gathered all the nations, and He will separate people one from another as a shepherd separates the sheep from the goats. And He will place the sheep on His right, but the goats on the left. Then the King will say to those on His

right, 'Come, you who are blessed by My Father, inherit the kingdom prepared for you from the foundation of the world'.
Then He will say to those on His left, 'Depart from me, you cursed, into the eternal fire prepared for the devil and his angels'." Matthew 25:31 - 34, 41 (ESV)

"Then I saw a great white throne and Him who was seated on it. From His presence earth and sky fled away, and no place was found for them. And I saw the dead, great and small, standing before the throne, and books were opened. Then another book was opened, which is the book of life. And the dead were judged by what was written in the books, according to what they had done. And the sea gave up the dead who were in it, Death and Hades gave up the dead who were in them, and they were judged, each one of them, according to what they had done. Then Death and Hades were thrown into the lake of fire. This is the second death, the lake of fire. And if anyone's name was not found written in the book of life, he was thrown into the lake of fire." Revelation 20:11 - 15 (ESV)

Process, Point, Process, Point: Salvation is a <u>process</u> by which God draws us to Him through circumstances and the conviction of the Holy Spirit. Then there is a <u>point</u> in time at which we believe and are justified and sealed by the Holy Spirit. We work out our salvation in the <u>process</u> of sanctification until we reach the final <u>point</u> of judgment and vindication by the blood of the Lamb along with receipt of a glorified body and participation in the kingdom of God.

The question of 'perseverance of the saints', or 'once saved always saved' still remains. Calvin notes that the perseverance of the saints is underpinned by election (and election is grounded in foreknowledge or omniscience: See Ephesians 1):

(Calvin:) "When Christ declares that He will by no means cast out one of those who do come unto Him; nay, that the life of all such is hidden and kept in security, in Himself, until He shall raise them up at the last day; who does not see here that <u>the final perseverance of the saints</u> (as it is commonly termed) is in like manner <u>ascribed to the election of God</u>? It may be, and has been, that <u>some fall from the faith</u>; but those who are given to Christ by the Father are, as Christ Himself declares, placed beyond the peril of destruction." (EPG, p. 36 - parenthetical note in original, underline is mine)

I understand Calvin to be using the word "faith" in this sentence to mean a system of belief or what we call "religion":

(Calvin:) "Every tree that my heavenly Father hath not planted, shall be rooted up." Whereby He plainly intimates, that the reprobate also sometimes take root, in appearance, and yet, are not planted by the hand of God." (EPG, p. 156)

Jesus may be describing those that "fall from the faith" in Matthew 13 as a "tare" or a "weed". These are people that "believe" there is a God, but never surrender or put their trust in Him. Believing in this context is nothing more than an intellectual assent that there is a God. Just as the demons believe there is a God and tremble:

"So also faith by itself, if it does not have works, is dead. But someone will say, "You have faith and I have works." Show me your faith apart from your works, and I will show you my faith by my works. You believe that God is one; you do well. Even the demons believe - - and shudder! Do you want to be shown, you foolish person, that faith apart from works is useless? Was not Abraham our father justified by works when he offered up his son Isaac on the altar? You see that faith was active along with his works, and faith was completed by his works; and the Scripture was fulfilled that says, "Abraham believed God, and it was counted to him as righteousness"--and he was called a friend of God. You see that a person is justified by works and not by faith alone." James 2:17 - 24 (ESV - underline is mine)

In *Christian Behavior*, which is book three in *Mere Christianity*, Chapters 11 and 12 are both titled "FAITH". C. S. Lewis does a far better job of explaining the relationship between faith and works in regards to salvation that I could ever hope to. You should read the chapters for yourself, but I will string a few sentences together to give the sense of what he says:

(Lewis:) "We cannot discover our failure to keep God's law except by trying our very hardest (and then failing). All this trying leads up to the vital moment at which you turn to God and say, 'You must do this. I can't.' It is the change from being confident about our own efforts to the state in which we despair of doing anything for ourselves and leave it to

God. I know the words 'leave it to God' can be misunderstood, but they must stay for the moment. The sense in which a Christian leaves it to God is that he puts all his trust in Christ: trusts that Christ will somehow share with him the perfect human obedience which He carried out from His birth to His crucifixion: that Christ will make the man more like Himself and, in a sense, make good his deficiencies. And, in yet another sense, handing everything over to Christ does not, of course, mean that you stop trying. To trust Him means, of course, trying to do all that He says. There would be no sense in saying you trusted a person if you would not take his advice. Christians have often disputed as to whether what leads the Christian home is good actions, or Faith in Christ. I have no right really to speak on such a difficult question, but it does seem to me like asking which blade in a pair of scissors is most necessary. A serious moral effort is the only thing that will bring you to the point where you throw up the sponge. Faith in Christ is the only thing to save you from despair at that point: and out of that Faith in Him good actions must inevitably come." (MC, p. 81 - Abridged)

I think it should be clear by this point that it is God who does all the "work" at the point of justification in salvation:

"I give them eternal life, and they will never perish, and no one will snatch them out of my hand. My Father, who has given them to me, is greater than all, and no one is able to snatch them out of the Father's hand. I and the Father are one." John 10:28 - 30 (ESV)

Those that believe that predestination is based upon foreknowledge will be correct in saying that you can take yourself out of the Father's hand and no longer have eternal life. They note that this verse only teaches that no one else is able to snatch you out of the Father's hand. You do not snatch yourself out; Instead, you will your salvation away, and deliberately forfeit eternal life. This is the peril of salvation based on God's foreknowledge of your faith. If it is your faith that puts you in, your confidence in your salvation is only as good as how confident you are in your continued faith. This is why C. S. Lewis and scripture teach that it is believing/faith that accepts the gift of salvation that is given by grace. It was Jesus that did the "work" of atoning for your sins. We do the believing. Jesus does the justifying. He is the one that puts you into His hand and gives you eternal, not temporary, life.

"For which I was appointed a preacher and apostle and teacher, which is why I suffer as I do. But I am not ashamed, for I know whom I have believed, and <u>I am convinced that He is able to guard until that Day what I have entrusted to Him</u>." 2 Timothy 1:11 -12 (ESV - footnote version - underline is mine)

Once again scripture teaches that those who believe and put their trust in the finished work of Christ, have the confidence that their salvation is secure in the hands of Jesus Himself. It is Jesus that is guarding the gift of eternal life that believers have been given. This verse also illustrates the opposing view that Calvinists hold. The following is the same verse in the text in the ESV (which is sometimes referred to as the Reformed Standard Version), rather than the more literal translation found in the footnote of the ESV, and most other versions of the Bible:

"But I am not ashamed, for I know whom I have believed, and I am convinced that he is able to guard until that Day <u>what has been entrusted to me</u>."

This change in the verse supports the Reformed belief in coercive monergism. Instead of putting our trust in Jesus: faith, repentance, justification, and eternal life are given or entrusted to the elect.

"I write these things to you who believe in the name of the Son of God that you may know that you have eternal life." 1 John 5:13 (ESV)

If you believe predestination is based on foreknowledge, you have to put your confidence in your ability to persevere in your faith. If you believe predestination is independent of foreknowledge, you have to hope that the faith you have is actually a gift from God, and not your own attempts to join a religion. If you 'fall away' from the church, or fail to persevere to the end, your former cell mates will simply say that you were never saved, as R. C. Sproul explains:

(Sproul:) "If we have it we never lose it; if we lose it we never had it." (CBG, p. 180)

If you believe that predestination is according to foreknowledge, you put your confidence in Jesus to guard the gift of eternal life He gave you when you put your trust in Him. You put your confidence in the sealing of the Holy Spirit, and the guarantee of your future inheritance. You can actually know right now that you have eternal life:

(Calvin:) "Believers ought to rest in the certainty of their salvation." (EPG, p. 124)

(Calvin:) "The Holy Spirit, therefore, nowhere exhorts us to the care and exercise of prayer, under any idea, that our salvation fluctuates in a state of uncertainty or doubt: for it rests safely in the hand of God." (EPG, p. 125)

Now that the riddle of the Reformation has been solved, perhaps the Calvinists and Arminians can cease their arguing. Protestants can apologize to Roman Catholics, and Roman Catholics can reconsider salvation by grace through faith - not by works but inevitably with works. Imagine what the Church can accomplish when the saints unite and press on to Orthopraxy:

"Religion that is pure and undefiled before God, the Father, is this: to visit orphans and widows in their affliction, and to keep oneself unstained from the world." James 1:27 (ESV)

APPENDIX ONE: CREEDS

THE APOSTLES CREED

I believe in God the Father Almighty: Creator of Heaven and earth.
And in Jesus Christ, His only Son, our Lord;
Who was conceived by the Holy Spirit, born of the Virgin Mary,
Suffered under Pontius Pilate, was crucified, dead, and buried;
He descended into hell; on the third day He rose again from the dead;
He ascended into Heaven, where He sits at the right hand of God the
Father Almighty;
From thence He shall come to judge the living and the dead.
I believe in the Holy Spirit,
One holy catholic Church,
The communion of the saints,
The forgiveness of sins,
The resurrection of the body,
And life everlasting.

THE NICENE CREED

We believe in one God, the Father Almighty, maker of heaven and earth,
and of all things visible and invisible. And in one Lord Jesus Christ, the
only begotten Son of God, and born of the Father before all ages. (God of
God) light of light, true God of true God. Begotten not made,
consubstantial to the Father, by whom all things were made. Who for us
men and for our salvation came down from heaven. And was incarnate of
the Holy Spirit and of the Virgin Mary and was made man; was crucified
also for us under Pontius Pilate, suffered and was buried; and the third
day rose again according to the Scriptures. And ascended into heaven, sits
at the right hand of the Father, and shall come again with glory to judge
the living and the dead, of whose Kingdom there shall be no end. And (I
believe) in the Holy Spirit, the Lord and Giver of life, who proceeds from
the Father (and the Son), who together with the Father and the Son is to
be adored and glorified, who spoke by the Prophets. And one holy,
catholic, and apostolic Church. We confess one baptism for the remission
of sins. And we look for the resurrection of the dead and the life of the
world to come. Amen.

THE ATHANASIAN CREED

Whosoever will be saved, before all things it is necessary that he hold the Catholic Faith. Which Faith except everyone do keep whole and undefiled, without doubt he shall perish everlastingly. And the Catholic Faith is this, that we worship one God in Trinity and Trinity in Unity. Neither confounding the Persons, nor dividing the Substance. For there is one Person of the Father, another of the Son, and another of the Holy Spirit. But the Godhead of the Father, of the Son and of the Holy Spirit is all One, the Glory Equal, the Majesty Co-Eternal. Such as the Father is, such is the Son, and such is the Holy Spirit. The Father Uncreated, the Son Uncreated, and the Holy Spirit Uncreated. The Father Incomprehensible, the Son Incomprehensible, and the Holy Spirit Incomprehensible. The Father Eternal, the Son Eternal, and the Holy Spirit Eternal and yet they are not Three Eternals but One Eternal. As also there are not Three Uncreated, nor Three Incomprehensibles, but One Uncreated, and One Uncomprehensible. So likewise the Father is Almighty, the Son Almighty, and the Holy Spirit Almighty. And yet they are not Three Almighties but One Almighty.

So the Father is God, the Son is God, and the Holy Spirit is God. And yet they are not Three Gods, but One God. So likewise the Father is Lord, the Son Lord, and the Holy Spirit Lord. And yet not Three Lords but One Lord. For, like as we are compelled by the Christian verity to acknowledge every Person by Himself to be God and Lord, so are we forbidden by the Catholic Religion to say, there be Three Gods or Three Lords. The Father is made of none, neither created, nor begotten. The Son is of the Father alone; not made, nor created, but begotten. The Holy Spirit is of the Father, and of the Son neither made, nor created, nor begotten, but proceeding.

So there is One Father, not Three Fathers; one Son, not Three Sons; One Holy Spirit, not Three Holy Spirits. And in this Trinity none is afore or after Other, None is greater or less than Another, but the whole Three Persons are Co-eternal together, and Co-equal. So that in all things, as is aforesaid, the Unity in Trinity, and the Trinity in Unity, is to be worshipped. He therefore that will be saved, must thus think of the Trinity.

Furthermore, it is necessary to everlasting Salvation, that he also believe rightly the Incarnation of our Lord Jesus Christ. For the right Faith is, that we believe and confess, that our Lord Jesus Christ, the Son of God, is God and Man. God, of the substance of the Father, begotten before the worlds; and Man, of the substance of His mother, born into the world. Perfect God and Perfect Man, of a reasonable Soul and human Flesh subsisting. Equal to the Father as touching His Godhead, and inferior to the Father as touching His Manhood. Who, although He be God and Man, yet He is not two, but One Christ. One, not by conversion of the Godhead into Flesh, but by taking of the Manhood into God. One altogether, not by confusion of substance, but by Unity of Person. For as the reasonable soul and flesh is one Man, so God and Man is one Christ. Who suffered for our salvation, descended into Hell, rose again the third day from the dead. He ascended into Heaven, He sits on the right hand of the Father, God Almighty, from whence He shall come to judge the quick and the dead. At whose coming all men shall rise again with their bodies, and shall give account for their own works. And they that have done good shall go into life everlasting, and they that have done evil into everlasting fire. This is the Catholic Faith, which except a man believe faithfully and firmly, he cannot be saved.

APPENDIX TWO: PHILOSOPHY

"Come now, let us reason together, says the LORD."
Isaiah 1:18

Philosophy: The rational investigation of the truths and principles of being, knowledge, or conduct. (Dictionary.com)

In short, everyone has a philosophy, whether they have thought it through or not. Our philosophy is the framework through which we look at the world. I like to think of this framework as a set of filters in our mind. When we experience something, we run the experience through this set of filters to reach a conclusion or derive some sort of meaning. C. S. Lewis gives an excellent account of how this works.

(Lewis:) "What we learn from experience depends on the kind of philosophy we bring to experience. It is therefore useless to appeal to experience before we have settled, as well as we can, the philosophical question." (Miracles, p. 211) "The result of our historical enquiries thus depends on the philosophical views which we have been holding before we even began to look at the evidence. This philosophical question must therefore come first." (Miracles, p. 211)

C. S. Lewis gives an example of how we can arrive at a forgone conclusion if we do not examine the philosophical framework we are using to determine the facts:

(Lewis:) "Here is an example of the sort of thing that happens if we omit the preliminary philosophical task, and rush on to the historical. In a popular commentary on the Bible you will find a discussion of the date at which the Fourth Gospel was written. The author says it must have been written after the execution of St. Peter, because, in the Fourth Gospel, Christ is represented as predicting the execution of St. Peter. 'A book', thinks the author, 'cannot be written *before* events which it refers to'. Of course it cannot -- unless real predictions ever occur. If they do, then his argument for the date is in ruins. And the author has not discussed at all whether real predictions are possible. He takes it for granted (perhaps

153

unconsciously) that they are not. Perhaps he is right: but if he is, he has not discovered this principle by historical inquiry. He has brought his disbelief in predictions to his historical work, so to speak, ready made. Unless he had done so his historical conclusion about the date of the Fourth Gospel could not have been reached at all. His work is therefore quite useless to a person who wants to know *whether* predictions occur. The author gets to work only after he has already answered that question in the negative, and on grounds which he never communicates to us." (Miracles, p. 211 - 212 - italics in original)

R.C. Sproul gives an excellent description of the shared philosophy of Calvin and C. S. Lewis. This is the orthodox philosophy about God, and since it is about God, it is tempting to call it theology instead of philosophy. This philosophy began with Augustine but was systematized by Thomas Aquinas in his *Summa Theologica*:

(Sproul:) "When we consider love as an attribute of God, we recognize that it is defined in relation to all the other attributes of God. This is true not only of love but also of every other attribute of God. It is important to remember that when we speak of the attributes of God, we are speaking of properties that cannot be reduced to composite parts. One of the first affirmations we make about the nature of God is that He is not a composite being. Rather we confess that God is a simple being. This does not mean that God is 'easy' in the sense that a simple task is not a difficult task. Here simplicity is not contrasted with difficulty but with composition. A being who is composite is made up of definite parts. As a human creature, I am composed of many parts, such as arms, legs, eyes, ears, lungs, etc."
"As a simple being, God is not made up of parts as we are. This is crucial to any proper understanding of the nature of God. This means that God is not partly immutable, partly omniscient, partly omnipotent, or partly infinite. He is not constructed of a section or segment of being that is then added to other sections or segments to comprise the whole of God. It is not so much that God has attributes but rather that He is His attributes. In simple terms (as distinct from difficult terms) this means that all of God's attributes help define all of His other attributes. For example, when we say God is immutable, we are also saying that His immutability is an eternal immutability, an omnipotent immutability, a holy immutability, a loving immutability, etc. By the same token His love is an immutable

love, an eternal love, an omnipotent love, a holy love, etc." (Loved, pp. 6 - 7)

The following section is a brief history of philosophy. If you take the time to grasp the following descriptions, you will be able to better understand the two dominant philosophies of our secular world: Pantheism and Naturalism. Parmenides, argued for *Monism* (*Mono* = One). There are two branches of monism (what Lewis calls *Everythingism*):

(Lewis:) "Thus the Everythingist, if he starts from God, becomes a Pantheist; there must be nothing that is not God. If he starts from Nature he becomes a Naturalist; there must be nothing that is not Nature." (Miracles, p. 301)

(Geisler:) "Parmenides, born circa 515 B.C. argued that all is one, because to assume that more than one thing exists is absurd. If there were two or more things, they would have to differ, but the only ways to differ are by something (being) or by nothing (non-being). However, it is impossible to differ by nothing, since to differ by nothing (or nonbeing) is just another way of saying there is no difference at all. And two things cannot differ by being because being (or existence) is the only thing they have in common- it is impossible to differ by the very respect in which they are the same. Hence, <u>Parmenides concluded that it is impossible to have two or more things. There can be only one being: All is one</u>, <u>and one is all</u>. Thus, whatever else appears to be does not really exist.
Put in the context of creation, this simply means that God exists and the world does not; there is a creator, but not really any creation. Or, at least, the only sense in which there can be said to be a creation is that it comes out of God the way a dream comes from a mind. The universe is only the nothing of which God thinks. God is the totality of all reality, and the non-real about which he thinks and which appears to us, like zero, does not exist. It is literally nothing.
The famous Hindu philosopher Shankara described the relation of the world to God, illusion to reality, by the analogy of what appears to be a snake but on closer examination turns out actually to be a rope. When we look at the world, what is there is not reality; rather it is merely an illusion. Likewise when a person looks at himself, what appears to be (body) is only an illusory manifestation of what really is (soul). And

when one looks into his soul, he discovers that the depth of his soul is really the depth of the universe: <u>Man is God.</u> <u>To think we are not God is part of the illusion or dream from which we must awaken.</u> <u>Sooner or later we must discover that all comes from God, and all is God.</u>" (ST 2, pp. 427 - 428 - underline is mine)

Geisler summarizes monism:

(Geisler:) "There cannot be more than one thing (absolute Monism), for if there were two things, they would have to differ. For things to differ, they must differ either by being or by nonbeing. But since being is that which makes them identical, they cannot differ by being. Nor, on the other hand, can they differ by nonbeing, for nonbeing is nothing, and to differ by nothing is not to differ at all. Hence, there cannot be a plurality of beings (both God and creatures) but only one single indivisible being - a rigid monism." (ST 1, pp. 21 - 22)

This version of monism is called absolute pantheism since it begins with the presupposition that there is a god.

There are two ways to try and defeat the brilliance of Parmenides. One way is to have things differ by non-being, the other is to find a difference in the beings themselves.

The Atomists, (Leucippus and Democritus, circa 500-370 B.C.) contended that the principle separating one being (or atom) from another is absolutely nothing (non-being). They called this the Void. The atoms do not differ in their essence, but in the space they occupy, so each being occupies a different space in the Void, and the void is empty space or non-being. Parmenides would simply point out that to differ by absolutely nothing is to have absolutely no difference at all. And to have absolutely no difference is to be absolutely the same. (see ST 1, p. 22)

Plato, with the help of Parmenides, tried to use "relative nonbeing" as the principle of differentiation. He argued that nonbeing in some way exists. One being is distinct from another not by what it is, but by what it is not. For example, the chair is distinguished from everything else in the room in that it is not the table, the floor, the wall, etc. Parmenides would simply have asked whether there were any differences in the beings themselves. If there were not, then he would have insisted that all these beings must be identical. For the monist there are not many beings but only one. (see ST 1, pp. 22 - 23)

156

Aristotle argued that there is a plurality of 47 or 55 beings, or unmoved movers, that are separated from one another in their very being. Parmenides would ask Aristotle just how simple beings can differ in their very being. Things composed of form and matter can differ in that THIS particular matter is different from THAT matter, even though they have the same form. But how do pure forms (beings) differ from each other? They have no principle of differentiation. If there is no difference in their being, then their being is identical. Aristotle was unable to avoid monism. (see ST 1, p. 22 - 23)

Finally, Thomas Aquinas, like Aristotle, sought differences within the beings themselves. Aquinas believed that all finite beings -for example: angels and man- are composed in their very being, while God is an absolutely simple (indivisible) Being, and there can only be one such Being. God is infinite, all creatures are finite. God is pure actuality (Act), all creatures are composed of actuality (act) and potentiality. Hence, finite things differ from God in that they have a limiting potentiality; He does not. Finite things can differ from each other in whether their potentiality is completely actualized (as in angels) or whether it is being progressively actualized (as in humans). In all creatures their essence (is-ness) is really distinct from their existence (what-ness). In God, on the other hand, His essence and existence are identical. Since God is without all composition, His understanding is not distinct from His essence. Aquinas was not the first to make this distinction, but he was the first to make extensive use of it. Aquinas argues that existence is something other than essence, except in God, whose essence is His existence. Such a being must be one and unique, since multiplication of anything is only possible where there is a difference. Parmenides assumed that being is always understood in the same way, Aquinas saw that being is analogous -- being understood in similar but different ways. (see ST 1, p. 24)

The creator is absolutely simple in His being. God cannot become more loving, more powerful, more wise, more righteous, etc. God is in a state of perfection, and since He is perfect and immutable, He is unable to sin. Any attribute that is in the essence of God extends to every other attribute that is in the essence or being of God.

While God is simple, His creation is composed and has potentiality. A tree can be cut down, sawed into boards and made into a table and chairs. The same table and chairs can be cut up and made into a fire. Angels can become demons, or they can learn from the rebellion of Satan and gain an understanding of what happens when one sins. Man changes every day. We grow and age. We learn to think, speak, and do math. We have experiences which change us.

Let us take our ability to reason and look at a few scriptures and see how this actually works in practice:

Genesis 1: 1 - 3 "In the beginning, God created the heavens and the earth. The earth was without form and void, and darkness was over the face of the deep. And the Spirit of God was hovering over the face of the waters. And God said, "Let there be light," and there was light." (ESV)

John 1: 1- 3 "In the beginning was the Word, and the Word was with God, and the Word was God. He was in the beginning with God. All things were made through Him, and without Him was not any thing made that was made." (ESV - Erasmus and Calvin translate Logos as "the Speech" instead of as "the Word" --see Calvin's commentary on John 1)

The first passage shows the tri-unity of God. God (The Father) created, the Spirit of God (The Holy Spirit) was hovering over the face of the waters, and God said (God the Word), "Let there be light." It is the passage in John that identifies the Word of God as Jesus. From these two passages of scripture we get the theology of the "trinity" -- God as three persons. A few years ago I was having a discussion with a Mormon, and he said to me, "You Christians, are so silly. You believe a logical contradiction: that God is three persons in one person." My reply to him was rather simple. I explained to him that if I believed that God was one person and three persons at the same time and in the same sense, he was right that this was a logical contradiction and foolishness. However, the orthodox doctrine of the trinity is that God is three persons in one being (or essence), and that is not logically contradictory.

(Calvin:) "They said that there are three Hypostases, or Subsistence's, or Persons, in the one and simple essence of God." (Commentary on John 1:1)

Using our ability to reason, we read scripture and find the theology that God is described as Father, Word, and Spirit. We use reason to develop two philosophies: The first is that God is three persons in one person. The second is that God is three persons in one being. Using logic, we are able to know the first option is wrong since it violates the law of non-contradiction: (A is not non-A: God is not non-God: God is not the

Devil: No two contradictory statements can both be true at the same time and in the same sense.)

Orthodox Christianity uses what is revealed about God in scripture and agrees with the philosophy about God that is not logically contradictory: God is three persons in one being.

TERMS AND DEFINITIONS

Calvinism: Generally defined as the teachings of Augustine, Luther, and Calvin - which are called Reformed, since they were popularized during the Protestant Reformation in the 1500's. Specifically defined by the Five TULIP Points dealing with Soteriology, which were formulated at the Synod of Dort to rebuke the five points submitted by the followers of Arminius.

Classical Theism: God is simple in His essence, while His creation is composed or complex. Uses Divine Essentialism to determine which attributes of God are essential, or proper, to His essence. Based on the *Summa Theologica* by Thomas Aquinas. See the appendix on philosophy.

Divine Essentialism: Belief that the only attributes of God that are essential to His nature are those attributes that are proper to His nature prior to His creating anything.

Eschatology: Study of Last Things, or End Times.

Exclusivism: Salvation is restricted to those that God chooses to give the gift of faith to; thereby, adopting and regenerating them. God is able to give the gift of faith to all, compelling every person to be saved from eternal damnation, but chooses not to.

Inclusivism: The belief that when it comes to the eternal destination of each person, God will hold each person accountable for the amount of Revelation each individual person received.

Intellectualism: There is a natural law: Something is correct, therefore, God wills it. Also known as Thomism, after Thomas Aquinas.

Natural Law: There is an objective right and wrong which is consistent with the way the universe works.

Reformed: Those that follow the teachings of Augustine, Luther, and Calvin in the areas of Sovereignty, Grace, and Soteriology.

Solecism: An error. Something that is incorrect.

Soteriology: Salvation.

Voluntarism: God is to be conceived of as some form of will: What God wills is correct, because He willed it. Also known as Scotism, after John Duns Scotus.

CAST OF CHARACTERS IN CHRONOLOGICAL ORDER

Irenaeus: Disciple of Polycarp who was a disciple of the Apostle John. Bishop in what is now Lyon, France. A church father who wrote *Against Heresies*. (Circa: 125 - 202)

Augustine of Hippo: Calvinists consider Augustine to be the theological father of the Reformation. Bishop of Hippo in Algeria, Africa. Author of more than 100 separate titles. (November 13, 354 - August 28, 430)

Aquinas, Thomas: Italian priest of the Catholic Church in the Dominican Order. Author of *Summa Theologica* as well as other books and articles. (1225 - 1274) Philosopher and Theologian in the tradition of Scholasticism. Proponent of Natural theology and father of the Thomistic school of philosophy and theology.

Luther, Martin: Monk and teacher at Wittenberg University in Wittenberg, Germany. Posting of his *95 Theses* credited with sparking the Reformation. Author of numerous articles and books. (1483 - 1546)

Pighius, Albert: Dutch Roman Catholic Theologian. Author of several works against the Reformers. (1490 - 1542)

Calvin, John (French: Calvin, Jean): French theologian who moved to Switzerland following violent uprisings against protestants in France. Best known for his *Institutes of the Christian Religion* and his commentaries on the books of the Bible. (1509 - 1564) Yes, Calvin was Reformed and a Calvinist.

Warfield, Benjamin Breckinridge: Professor of Theology at Princeton Seminary. (1851 - 1921) Calvinist - Reformed.

Chesterton, Gilbert Keith: A prolific English writer and Christian Apologist. (1874 - 1936) Anglican, then converted to Roman Catholicism.

Lewis, Clive Staples: Teacher at Magdalen College in Oxford, England for thirty years. Professor of Medieval and Renaissance English at the

University of Cambridge. Author of numerous books. (1898 - 1963) Anglican - Church of England.

Geisler, Norman: Chair of Christian Apologetics at Veritas Evangelical Seminary in Murrieta, CA. Professor at several universities or seminaries for over 40 years. Author of over 50 books and numerous articles. (1932 -) Self described "moderate" Calvinist or Amyraldian.

Sproul, R. C.: Chairman of Ligonier Ministries. Author of over 60 books. (1939 -). Calvinist - Reformed.

Piper, John: Pastor of Bethlehem Baptist Church in Minneapolis, MN. Author of over 10 books. (1946 -) Calvinist - Reformed.

Mohler, Albert: President of Southern Baptist Theological Seminary in Louisville, KY. (1959 -). Calvinist - Reformed.

White, James: Director of Alpha and Omega Ministries in Phoenix, AZ. Author of over 20 books. (1962 -) Calvinist - Reformed.

BIBLIOGRAPHY

The first section gives the abbreviations used in the text of the book, the author, and title. The second section gives the complete citation for each work:

Abolition: Lewis, C. S. *The Abolition of Man.*

BC: Chesterton, G. K. *The Complete Father Brown Stories: The Blue Cross.*

Bondage: Luther, Martin. *The Bondage of the Will.*

CBF: Geisler, Norman. *Chosen But Free: A Balanced View of Divine Election.*

CBG: Sproul, R. C. *Chosen by God.*

EPG: Calvin, John. *A Treatise On The Eternal Predestination of God.*

ESV: English Standard Version

Five Points: Steele & Thomas. *The Five Points of Calvinism: Defined, Defended, Documented.*

KJV: King James Version

Loved: Sproul, R. C. *Loved by God.*

LTM: Lewis, C. S. *Letters To Malcolm: Chiefly on Prayer.*

MC: Lewis, C. S. *Mere Christianity.*

Miracles: Lewis, C. S. *Miracles.*

NIV: New International Version

NKJV: New King James Version

Perfectionism: Warfield, Benjamin Breckinridge. *Perfectionism.*

Perelandra: Lewis, C. S. *Perelandra.*

PF: White, James. *The Potter's Freedom.*

POP: Lewis, C. S. *The Problem of Pain.*

Reason: Geisler, Norman & Brooks, Ronald M. *Come, Let Us Reason. An Introduction to Logical Thinking.*

SBJ: Lewis, C. S. *Surprised by Joy.*

Silent: Lewis, C. S. *Out of the Silent Planet.*

Strength: Lewis, C. S. *That Hideous Strength.*

ST 1: Geisler, Norman. *Systematic Theology, Volume One.*

ST 2: Geisler, Norman. *Systematic Theology, Volume Two.*

ST 3: Geisler, Norman. *Systematic Theology, Volume Three.*

TGD: Lewis, C. S. *The Great Divorce.*

TLB: Lewis, C. S. *The Last Battle.*

TMN: Lewis, C. S. *The Magician's Nephew.*

Unspoken Sermons: MacDonald, George. *Unspoken Sermons, Series I, II,* and *III.*

VDT: Lewis, C. S. *The Voyage Of The Dawn Treader.*

WTB: Sproul, R. C. *Willing to Believe.*

Calvin, John. *A Treatise On The Eternal Predestination Of God.* (*A Defence Of The Secret Providence of God*). Originally published in

Geneva, Switzerland in 1552. Translated by Henry Cole in 1856 and titled: Calvin's Calvinism.

Chesterton, G. K. *The Complete Father Brown Stories*: *The Blue Cross*. Wordsworth Editions Limited. 2006. ISBN: 978-1-85326-003-2

Geisler, Norman. *Chosen But Free*: *A Balanced View of Divine Election*. (Second Edition). Bethany House Publishers. Bloomington, MN. 1999, 2001. ISBN: 0-7642-2521-9

Geisler, Norman & Brooks, Ronald M. *Come, Let Us Reason*: *An Introduction to Logical Thinking*. Baker Book House. Grand Rapids, MI. 1990, 2002. ISBN: 0-8010-3836-7

Geisler, Norman. *Systematic Theology, Volume One*. Bethany House Publishers. Bloomington, MN. 2002. ISBN: 0-7642-2551-0

Geisler, Norman. *Systematic Theology, Volume Two*. Bethany House Publishers. Bloomington, MN. 2003. ISBN: 0-7642-2552-9

Geisler, Norman. *Systematic Theology, Volume Three*. Bethany House Publishers. Bloomington, MN. 2004. ISBN: 0-7642-2553-7

Heschel, Abraham Joshua. *The Prophets*. Hendrickson Publishers, Inc. Peabody, MA. 2009. ISBN: 978-1-59856-181-4 Copyright 1962 by Abraham J. Heschel.

Lewis, C. S. *Letters To Malcolm*: *Chiefly On Prayer*. Harcourt, Inc. ISBN: 0-I5-602766-6 (pb.) Copyright 1964, 1963, C. S. Lewis Pte. Ltd. Copyright renewed 1992, 1991 by Arthur Owen Barfield.

Lewis, C. S. *The Chronicles of Narnia*. HarperCollins Publishers, New York, NY. ISBN: 0-06-059824-7
    The Magician's Nephew. Copyright 1955, C. S. Lewis Pte. Ltd.
    The Lion, The Witch And The Wardrobe. Copyright 1950, C. S. Lewis Pte. Ltd.
    The Horse and His Boy. Copyright 1954, C. S. Lewis Pte. Ltd.
    Prince Caspian. Copyright 1951, C. S. Lewis Pte. Ltd.
    The Voyage Of The Dawn Treader. Copyright 1952,

C. S. Lewis Pte. Ltd.
The Silver Chair. Copyright 1953, C. S. Lewis Pte. Ltd.
The Last Battle. Copyright 1956, C. S. Lewis Pte. Ltd.

Lewis, C. S. *The Complete C. S. Lewis Signature Classics*.
HarperSanFrancisco. ISBN: 0-06-050608-3
Mere Christianity. Copyright 1952, C. S. Lewis Pte. Ltd.
The Screwtape Letters. Copyright 1942, C. S. Lewis Pte. Ltd.
Miracles. Copyright 1947, C. S. Lewis Pte. Ltd.
The Great Divorce. Copyright 1946, C. S. Lewis Pte. Ltd.
The Problem of Pain. Copyright 1940, C. S. Lewis Pte. Ltd.
A Grief Observed. Copyright 1961, C. S. Lewis Pte. Ltd.
The Abolition of Man. Copyright 1944, C. S. Lewis Pte. Ltd.

Lewis, C. S. *Out of the Silent Planet*. Scribner. New York, NY. 2003.
ISBN: 978-0-7432-3490-0 Copyright 1938 by Clive Staples Lewis.

Lewis, C. S. *Perelandra*. Scribner. New York, NY. 2003. ISBN: 978-0-
7432-3491-7 Copyright 1944 by Clive Staples Lewis. Copyright 1972 by
Alfred Cecil Harwood and Arthur Owen Barfield.

Lewis, C. S. *That Hideous Strength*. Scribner. New York, NY. 2003.
ISBN: 978-0-7432-3492-4 Copyright 1945, 1946 by Clive Staples Lewis.
Copyright 1973, 1974 by Alfred Cecil Harwood and Arthur Owen
Barfield.

Lewis, C. S. *The Beloved Works of C. S. Lewis: Surprised by Joy:
Reflections on the Psalms: The Four Loves: The Business of Heaven*.
Inspirational Press. New York, NY. ISBN: 978-0-88486-445-5 Surprised
by Joy, copyright 1986, 1984 by Arthur Owen Barfield.

Luther, Martin. *The Bondage of the Will*. Henry Cole, translation. Baker.
1976.

MacDonald, George. *Unspoken Sermons, Series I, II*, and *III*. Feather
Trail Press.

Piper, John. *The Justification of God*. Baker Book House. Grand Rapids,
MI. 1993.

Sproul, R. C. *Chosen by God*. Tyndale House Publishers, Inc. Wheaton, IL. 1986. ISBN: 0-8423-0282-4

Sproul, R. C. *Loved by God*. Word Publishing. Nashville, TN. 2001 ISBN: 0-8499-1648-8

Sproul, R. C. *Willing to Believe*. Baker Book House. Grand Rapids, MI. 1997.

Steele, David N. & Thomas, Curtis C. *The Five Points of Calvinism: Defined, Defended, Documented*. Presbyterian & Reformed Publishing Co. Phillipsburg, NJ. 1963. ISBN: 0-87552-444-3

Warfield, Benjamin Breckinridge. *Perfectionism*. Presbyterian and Reformed Publishing Company, Philadelphia, PA. 1958.

White, James. *The Potter's Freedom*. Calvary Press Publishing. 2009. ISBN: 1-879737-43-4

Brothers, if anyone is caught in any transgression, you who are spiritual should restore him in a spirit of gentleness. Keep watch on yourself, lest you too be tempted. Galatians 6:1 (ESV)

Thank You for taking the time to read my book.
Any questions or comments will be appreciated:

Jordan Ferrier
10930 Skylane Court
Allendale, MI 49401
email: classicaltheist@yahoo.com

Foundation of Reformed Theology / Calvinism:

1. God is free to over-rule any of His creatures' decisions.

2.   A. God is Omniscient
          B. God is Omnipotent
          C. God is Perfect

3.   A. God knew the fall would happen.
          B. God could have stopped the fall from happening.
          C. God did not need to create anything.

4. The fall was willed, ordained, and decreed by God > Everything that happens is the will of God.

5. No free-will in man or angel.

6. Correct because God wills it. > Created for the Glory of God.

7. Man does not know what good is.

8. Total Depravity or Total Inability. > Three meanings of Faith.

9. Unconditional Election. > Predetermination independent of Foreknowledge.

10. Limited Atonement. > God able to save all - will save all that Jesus died for.

11. Irresistible Effectual Grace > Grace universal

12. Perseverance of the Saints. > Those that "fall from the faith" were never saved.

Foundation of Classical Theism:

1. God is free to give real freedom to His creatures.

2.   A. God is Omniscient
   B. God is Omnipotent
   C. God is Perfect

3.   A. God knew the fall would happen.
   B. God could not stop the fall from happening.
   C. God did not need to create anything.

4. The fall was not ordained by God > God chose to give man the ability to choose.

5. Man and Angel's are "Free Moral Agents".

6. Correct; Therefore, God wills it. > Man created so God could Love us.

7. The ability for man to know good and evil is impaired.

8. Unrighteous with impaired ability > Faith - ability to believe - common to all.

9. Election is Predetermined according to Foreknowledge

10. Universal, Voluntary, Particular, Penal, Substitutionary Atonement.

11. Universal Resistible Grace > Each person held responsible for the amount of revelation received.

12. Perseverance of the Saints. > Only the elect believe.

CPSIA information can be obtained at www.ICGtesting.com
Printed in the USA
LVOW06s2049300815

452107LV00031B/1608/P